Inclusive Practice

in

Inclusive Practice
Handbook

Supporting Special N̶e̶e̶d̶s̶ Foundation Stage

Ages
3–5

Dr Hannah Mortimer

Author
Dr Hannah Mortimer

Editor
Sally Gray

Series Designer
Rebecca Male

Design
Q2A Media

Illustrations
Debbie Clark

Cover Designer
Rebecca Male

Acknowledgements

Cover artwork © Comstock Inc.; Corel Corporation; Digitalstock/Corbis; Ingram Publishing; Jupiter Images; Photodisc Inc/Getty; Stockbyte.
Every effort has been made to trace copyright holders and the publishers apologise for any inadvertent omissions.

Text © 2007, Hannah Mortimer
© 2007, Scholastic Ltd

Designed using Adobe InDesign

Published by Scholastic Ltd, Villiers House,
Clarendon Avenue, Leamington Spa, Warwickshire CV32 5PR

Visit our website at www.scholastic.co.uk

Printed by Bell and Bain Ltd, Glasgow

1 2 3 4 5 6 7 8 9 0   7 8 9 0 1 2 3 4 5 6

British Library Cataloguing-in-Publication Data A catalogue record for this book is available from the British Library.

ISBN 978-0439-94563-9

Inclusive Practice Handbook

051430
371.9 Mar
CHILDCARE
INCLUSIVE EDUCATION
SHENSTONE

Introduction

This is the handbook for a new series aimed at helping you plan inclusive and flexible activities for children who have special educational needs in your setting. This section introduces the approach and describes what we mean by 'special educational needs'.

▲●■ The aims of the series

This new series aims to bring you up to date with what you need to know, in order to plan inclusive practice for the children you work with who have special educational needs (SEN) within the Early Years Foundation Stage (EYFS). This new series is a comprehensive look at the latest developments in Early Years education and specifically inclusive practice in the Early Years. It builds on the previous successful Early Years series *Special Needs in Early Years* (Scholastic) in which readers were introduced to their duties under the SEN Code of Practice. In the previous series, readers were shown how to plan activities that contributed towards the Early Learning Goals for all the children and yet which also carried specifically targeted learning outcomes for children who had special educational needs. In this new series the activities are linked to the EYFS and therefore cover a broader age range from 0 to 5 years. The activities contained in the three activity books in this series are also designed to contribute towards helping the children to achieve the Early Learning Goals. Because they are open-ended they can be used much more flexibly so that all colleagues can follow a child's 'play plan' when interacting and supporting a child with a given area of need. This approach is non-prescriptive and will help you to tune into the child's needs using general strategies for supporting all of the child's play and learning – planned or otherwise.

This handbook accompanies the series and covers the very basic information that you need to know in order to apply the SEN Code of Practice to your setting. It will guide you through the minor amendments or additions to the Code, namely the new terminology and the greater emphasis on inclusion and disability awareness. This handbook will bring you up to date on the recent changes and help you to see special educational needs in terms of removing barriers and personalising the children's learning. In this series there are also activity books on supporting these areas of special need in EYFS:

- Autistic spectrum disorder
- Behaviour, emotional and social difficulties
- Speech and language difficulties.

▲ ● ■ What is the SEN Code of Practice?

The aim in Early Years is to enable all children with SEN to reach their full potential, to be included fully and make a successful transition into school.

The SEN Code of Practice (DfES 2001) is a guide for school governors, registered early years settings and Local Authorities about the practical help they can give to children with special educational needs. It recommends that registered early years providers should identify children's needs and take action to meet those needs as early as possible, working with parents. The aim in Early Years is to enable all children with special educational needs to reach their full potential, to be included fully and make a successful transition into school. Children have special educational needs if they have a learning difficulty which calls for 'special educational provision' to be made. In turn, children have a 'learning difficulty' if they have a significantly greater difficulty in learning than the majority of children of the same age or a disability which prevents or hinders them from making use of the early years facilities locally available. In essence, children have SEN if their educational needs are 'additional or different' in some way.

▲ ● ■ Aims of this book

This book will be a helpful addition to your publications on inclusion and SEN and will be of most use to you if used flexibly and dipped into. It is impossible and inappropriate to provide 'recipe book' approaches for supporting SEN and the aim of this book is to tune you into the particular barriers faced in the EYFS by children who have special educational needs (SEN). It will help you to plan how you can change what you provide to include these children fully. Inclusion in its widest sense is: *a process of identifying, understanding and breaking down barriers to participation and learning* (this definition was devised by members of the Early Childhood Forum in 2003).

▲ ● ■ How the handbook is organised

The first chapter in this handbook considers inclusive practice and what it actually means for the practitioner and for the children that he or she works with. The distinction between a medical and a social model of disability is examined and this chapter also considers how to plan inclusive activities that help to remove the barriers for these children. Chapter Two takes a look at some of the children

concerned and contains a potted version of the range of needs covered in this series as well as some general information about some other areas of need.

Chapter Three provides a reminder of the practitioner's duties under the SEN Code of Practice. Chapter Four considers how to identify and support SEN within the broad framework of the EYFS. For example, there are new duties under disability legislation which are introduced and explained. In this chapter there is also a description of the 'Assessment-planning-evaluation model' used in the activity books of this series, including an insight into how this might work for one child.

Chapter Five explores the role of the SENCO and offers ideas for developing an inclusion policy for an early years setting.

Chapter Six provides plenty of ideas to help practitioners plan inclusive play opportunities for all children, working within the EYFS framework. It offers suggestions for sharing approaches with colleagues and helpers. Chapter Seven is devoted to ways of ensuring children's participation and 'listening' to their needs and views, whatever their age or level of ability. To facilitate work with parents and carers, other professionals and agencies, Chapter Eight provides practical ideas about partnership and communication with others. Finally, is a list of resources and further reading at the end of the book (page 63).

▲ ● ■ Working within the EYFS framework

The EYFS (introduced from 2008) provides a statutory framework for schools and registered early years settings who cater for children up to the end of the school year in which they reach their fifth birthday. How can you work within the EYFS to meet the SEN of the children you work with and care for? The revised framework provides a method of personalising all children's learning. In other words, the best approaches for each child (whether or not with SEN) will be those that are individually designed, personalised to their particular way of learning and based upon the child's strengths, weaknesses, experiences and needs.

The non-statutory practice guidance for the EYFS sets out detailed assessment suggestions in the 'Look, listen and note' sections of the Learning and Development grids. Within these, you can see the kinds of pathways that children typically show through their first five years as they make progress towards the Early Learning Goals. They are not rigidly fixed or sequenced and not intended as a curriculum in themselves. You are expected to make systematic observations and assessments of each child's achievements, interests and learning styles. You should then use these to identify learning priorities and plan relevant and motivating learning experiences for each child. Finally, you should match your observations to the expectations of the Early Learning Goals, both in your ongoing observations and with the EYFS Profile completed at the end of the EYFS period. Ongoing assessment is an integral part of the learning and development process and should be based on your observations of what the children are doing in their day-to-day activities. An ongoing dialogue with parents and carers should ensure that information about progress is shared and that everyone contributes to this continual assessment of progress.

▲ ● ■ A new approach for SEN

The same 'Look, listen and note' format has been developed in the activity books for this series, adapted for children who have certain SEN. Although practitioners should use the same ongoing assessment for children who have SEN as for any other child, it can sometimes be difficult to know what to look out for in particular and this is where the suggestions in the activity books can help.

If you work with children who have SEN, you might find that the developmental pathways described in the Learning and Development grids are not typical for children who have that kind of difficulty; or that the developmental steps

> In other words, the best approaches for each child (whether or not with SEN) will be those that are individually designed, personalised to their particular way of learning and based upon the child's strengths, weaknesses, experiences and needs.

described are too great to be meaningful. Within the activity books in this series, there are suggestions for ways to break down the steps, helping you to tune into the different pathways that children who have Autistic spectrum disorder, speech and language difficulties (SLD) or behaviour, social or emotional difficulties (BESD) might follow. Once again, it is important to remember that each child is unique and that these pathways cannot be used rigidly. However, being aware of how these children's needs might differ from other children's should provide you with the confidence to use your observations and planning flexibly. After all, we know that, in practical terms, SEN is simply defined as 'needs which are additional or different'.

▲ ● ■ Effective practice for SEN

Another challenge for those of you working with SEN is to fit what you have learned about a child's SEN into your statutory requirement to work within the EYFS framework. How can you 'match observations to the expectations of the Early Learning Goals' if these children are learning differently and requiring additional support? Again, this series is an attempt to do just that. Each activity book considers an area of SEN (such as ASD) and helps you to break down the EYFS framework into pathways and steps that the child can manage successfully. Within each book, six particular focuses are selected (such as 'Dispositions and attitudes'), each corresponding to the Areas of Learning and selected because children with that particular SEN might be particularly challenged. You are helped to see how the pathways lead on to the Early Learning Goals which a child with SEN might or might not achieve within the time frame of the EYFS. Assessment sheets allow you to focus in on the stage of development that a child has reached and there are examples of 'play plans' that break down some of these steps into practical ideas and suggestions for support.

> Another challenge for those of you working with SEN is to fit what you have learned about a child's SEN into your statutory requirement to work within the EYFS framework.

The 'Effective practice' sections of the EYFS Learning and Development grids are also a feature of the activity books as you read about the particular approaches that might be helpful. It is intended that you will find this new approach helpful and easy to follow, giving you the confidence to design your own pathways and play plans for other Areas of Learning, using some of the photocopiable templates in the books.

▲ ● ■ Early Support

You will find many references to the government initiative of Early Support in this book (www.earlysupport.org.uk). This initiative provides a framework for working in partnership with families and other professionals and a really useful set of resources for families who have young disabled children. There is also a helpful on-line resource for early years practitioners – visit www.standards.dfes.gov.uk/eyfs. The website helps you to break down the EYFS 'Development matters', 'Look, listen and note' and 'Effective practice' aspects of the Areas of Learning into finer steps. Look out for the additional 'Early Support' material on the site – this gives practical help for practitioners needing to observe children's development more closely and to plan for individualised learning for children who are developing more slowly or who need more consolidation of learning before moving on.

Organisations

- ADHD Family Support Group, 1A High Street, Dilton Marsh, Westbury, Wiltshire BA14 4DL.
- Association for Spina Bifida and Hydrocephalus, ASBAH House, 42 Park Road, Peterborough PE1 2UQ. Tel: 01733 555988 www.asbah.org
- Barnardo's (provides care and support for children in need and their families, with projects throughout the UK), Tanners Lane, Barkingside, Ilford, Essex IG6 1QG.
Tel: 020 8550 8822 www.barnardos.org.uk
- 'Contact a Family' (produces on subscription the 'CaF Directory of specific conditions and rare syndromes in children with their family support networks'),
209-211 City Road, London EC1V 1JN. Tel: 020 7608 8700 www.cafamily.org.uk
- The Department for Education and Skills (DfES) (for parent information and for Government circulars and advice including the SEN Code of Practice) www.dfes.gov.uk
- The Down's Syndrome Association, Langdon Down Centre, 2a Langdon Park, Teddington TW11 9PS. Tel: 0845 230 0372 www.dsa-uk.com
- The Dyspraxia Foundation, 8 West Alley, Hitchin SG5 1EG. Tel: 01462 454986 www.dyspraxiafoundation.org.uk
- Early Support (for general information and all the parent materials) www.earlysupport.org.uk
- Makaton Vocabulary Development Project (information about Makaton sign vocabulary and training), 31 Firwood Drive, Camberley, Surrey GU15 3QD.
- MENCAP (a support organisation for children with severe learning difficulties and their families) www.mencap.org.uk
- The National Autistic Society, 393 City Road, London, EC1V 1NG. Helpline: 0845 070 4004 www.nas.org.uk
- National Children's Bureau (A multi-disciplinary organisation concerned with the promotion and identification of the interests of all children and young people. Involved in research, policy and practice development, and consultancy), 8 Wakley Street, London EC1V 7QE www.ncb.org.uk
- National Council of Voluntary Child Care Organisations (Umbrella group for voluntary organisations dealing with children. Ensuring the wellbeing and safeguarding of children and families and maximising the voluntary sector's contribution to the provision of services), Unit 4, Pride Court, 80-82 White Lion Street, London N1 9PF. Tel: 020 7833 3319 www.ncvcco.org
- The Royal National Institute for the Blind, 224 Great Portland Street, London W1N 6AA. Send an sae for their pamphlet and resource list, 'The early years'.
- RNID, Information line (freephone): 0808 808 0123 www.rnid.org.uk
- SCOPE (for resources relating to children and adults who have cerebral palsy), 12 Park Crescent, London W1N 4EQ. Helpline: (freephone) 0800 626216 www.scope.org.uk

Inclusive Practice

If we are to include children who have SEN fully in the EYFS, we have to understand that each and every child learns differently and adapt what we do to ensure that they can access the curriculum.

▲ ● ■ Children learning differently

> It is up to us to identify any barriers they might face when accessing our curriculum and to plan adaptations flexibly.

Each child is unique, each is special and each will learn in a different way. Getting to know the individual learning styles and assessing the individual needs of the children allows you to personalize their learning experiences so that each and every one can make progress. We all know of children who are primarily lookers, listeners or doers. We also know that most children in their early years are a delightful mixture of all three, busily making connections between their experiences and their senses as they play and learn. If you have reached the point of seeing each child as having a very individual learning style, then you are well placed to see children who have SEN simply as an extension of this. They will have their own individual package of strengths and weaknesses and might need more of your support than others. The guidelines within the SEN Code of Practice suggest a very pragmatic view of SEN – in a nutshell, children have SEN if their needs are additional or different to the majority of the other children. It is up to us to identify any barriers they might face when accessing our curriculum and to plan adaptations flexibly.

▲ ● ■ The evolution of inclusion

The word 'inclusion' has developed and widened its meaning over the past few years. It means far more than including children with SEN and disability and also refers to including people generally regardless of ability, gender, race, religion and age – in fact, as a term it is still developing. We are moving towards better inclusion for children with disabilities and SEN and also recognition that we should ensure equal opportunities for all the children in our care. Members of the Early Childhood Forum have devised this very dynamic definition: *Inclusion is a process of identifying, understanding and breaking down barriers to participation and belonging.*

▲ ● ■ A medical model

In the past, assessing special educational needs involved the identification and remediation of children's deficits and defects. If we focus on a young child's disabilities or deficits, there is a tendency to lose sight of what is most important for learning and development during the early childhood years – that is, opportunities to engage successfully in a variety of playful interactions with people and objects in one's environment. The traditional notion in special education that simply identifying them and 'fixing them' in some way can resolve educational difficulties has not borne fruit and could be seen as personally offensive. This is known as a 'medical model' of disability and SEN.

▲ ● ■ A competent child

By focusing on a child's competencies and strengths, it becomes possible to remove the barriers that young children with SEN often experience in their attempts to

play and interact. Environments can be adapted and activities can be devised to develop the child's competencies in play, social interaction and exploration. As the philosophy of providing education inclusively begins to permeate, we are likely to see more emphasis on adjusting approaches to suit children, rather than placing children in different settings depending on whether or not they can 'cope'. Already we are seeing the dawn of new policies for inclusion which, in turn, are developing into more inclusive practice in early years settings. This change is happening from 'coal face up' as well as 'top down', as early years educators themselves begin to reflect on their practice and translate their own philosophies of inclusion into good practice with their children.

▲ ● ■ Keeping it practical

Here are some practical ways in which you can make play and learning approaches accessible for all children wherever possible.

• Try not to have 'special' activities for 'special' children or to buy plenty of 'special needs' equipment as this does not help the development of an inclusive provision.

• So often, an activity can be changed in some way rather than excluding certain children from it because they cannot 'fit in' with it. Flexible approaches and adaptable timetables and routines make this easier.

• Outdoor play areas need to contain quiet, sheltered spaces as well as busy active areas.

• Indoors, tables and equipment need to be at adjustable heights and floor spaces must be comfortable and safe to play on.

• Acoustics can be softened with soft surfaces, cushions, carpets and curtains, making it easier for everyone to hear clearly.

• Story times can be kept concrete by using props and visual aids.

• Communication can be enhanced by making sure that all adults at the setting are familiar with any language or communication systems used by the children.

• Children can also have a communication book showing how they make their needs known. You will find an idea for a 'child passport' on page 61.

• Make more use of colours, textures and smells to encourage different senses and to develop sensory play.

• Look for ways of making tools and equipment easy to handle by all children, such as by using foam padding wrapped around paintbrushes to make them easier to hold, or providing non-slip mats to hold small toys into position.

• Throughout the EYFS, look out for materials, pictures and books that portray positive images of disabled people and special needs.

▲ ● ■ Getting to know you

When you are welcoming a child with SEN to your setting, start by finding out all you need to know in order to help that child settle and make progress. Talking to parents and carers is an obvious starting point. They are experts on their own child and will have a great deal of information to offer you if you can ask the right questions. Many very young children who have complex and long-term

needs now receive Early Support. This is a recent government programme for ensuring that parents and carers receive joined-up support from the earliest opportunity (visit www.earlysupport.org.uk). A key worker is appointed to work with the family and there are family-held records through which they can tell their own story once without repeating it to every professional who calls. Find out if the child you are working with is on Early Support and contact the key worker if that is so.

▲ ● ■ What you can do

Here are some simple methods for getting to know the children quickly.

• If the policy for your setting allows it, home visits are an excellent way to get to know children on their own territories before you work and play together in the setting. They are a way of gathering information and also giving the child, the family and yourself greater confidence. Make sure you look after you own safety and follow the 'lone worker' guidelines that your organisation should have.

• Use a 'Welcome' form or 'Child passport' to gather information about a child's likes and dislikes, how the child makes their needs known and what level of support the child needs from you throughout your regular routines and activities. You will find more ideas on page 61.

• Now that you have met and found out more about the child, think through your typical session from a child's-eye-view. Think about each part of your routine (arrival, drinks, selecting activities, group time, and so on) and visualise the barriers that this child might face in accessing that activity. What needs to change? What would work really well? Take a walk around your spaces – are they child-friendly for this particular child?

• Plan the first few days carefully – a lot of people's confidences hang on these going successfully! Make a point of keeping closely in touch with the family throughout this period so that you can share 'good news' long before you need to share any concerns.

• Play alongside the child as often as you can so that you develop a 'feel' for how the child learns and behaves. This will help you to form a positive relationship together.

• Once the child has settled, stand back a little in order to observe and assess the level of support needed.

▲ ● ■ Positive attitudes

> One of the first ways of developing more inclusive practice in your setting is to examine your attitudes and beliefs and make sure that any barriers that might be caused by uncertainty or lack of confidence are removed.

One of the first ways of developing more inclusive practice in your setting is to examine your attitudes and beliefs and make sure that any barriers that might be caused by uncertainty or lack of confidence are removed.

• Be positive about everything a child can achieve. Try to focus on what children can do instead of what they cannot. This will also help you to develop a close working partnership with parents and carers. Above all, avoid giving the message that early learning carries an element of 'pass or fail' so that three and four-year olds never end up saying, 'I can't…'

• Look on each child as an individual. What works for one child might not work for another, even if both happen to have the same medical condition. Use what you can find out about a child's condition to inform your teaching and support but be prepared to use the information flexibly and to adapt it in the light of what you find out about the individual child.

• Focus on the whole child and not just that part of the child with additional needs. Remember that the child has joined your setting for wide and balanced EYFS opportunities and not just to have needs met in a narrow area. Early Years education is, after all, your area of specialism – so enjoy working and playing with the child rather than worrying about not being a specialist in the child's condition.

• Celebrate children playing and learning, rather than seeing success in terms of finished products. Each child will take a different pathway in their learning and you are there to support the processes involved rather than the 'fixed' product. This is why you must use the assessment sheets and play plans in the activity books flexibly and not see them as curricula in themselves.

• Respect the dignity of choice. You might feel tempted to be over-protective of a child who has SEN but try to offer choices wherever possible and encourage independence and initiative.

▲ ● ■ Aim for inclusive teaching strategies

Since each child will be following a different pathway through the EYFS, aim to set learning objectives and select teaching strategies that make sense for that individual child's needs and potential barriers to learning.

• Make sure that your teaching strategies match the preferred learning style for the child concerned. For many children this will involve using a multi-sensory approach to teaching and learning, making sure that you provide opportunities for children to make links between seeing, hearing and doing.

• Try not to overload children with complicated activities or too much new information at once. Keep your approaches simple and break activities down into shorter tasks if you need to.

• Aim for fail-proof learning so that the child is bound to succeed. Usually this involves providing just the right level of support and making step sizes sufficiently small for a child to manage successfully whatever their needs.

• Make the most of routines so that all children know what is expected of them. This will help them to feel settled and supported in your environment. Visual timetables of what is going to happen next and the use of objects of reference (such as a cup to signal 'drinks time') are useful ways of achieving this.

• Ensure that activities and outings are inclusive. If anyone is likely to be left out, change the activity or the outing!

• Monitor transitions carefully. This means being especially aware of how children manage arrivals, departures and changes of activity within the session. It also means looking very carefully at transition into school or other settings so that information flows smoothly between you all, and the child is helped to settle in.

▲ ● ■ Removing physical barriers

Settings need to be aware of ensuring physical access not only for children with disabilities – but for parents, visitors and staff members who might find access difficult.

• Take advice from your Local Authority if you are still concerned about the physical access to your buildings, including ramps, parking bays and wide entrances.

• Remove clutter where possible. If you have rather a lot of chairs, consider whether floor cushions might serve just as well. Make sure that everything has a set place to be tidied away to at the end of the session. Encourage children to be aware of obstacles and help them to move around freely.

• Be aware of your floor surfaces. Some children may not be walking yet and need clean surfaces for crawling and creeping. At the same time, a range of different floor surfaces helps children with sensory difficulties to 'map' their surroundings through feeling the floor texture or hearing the quality of the echoing sounds.

• Provide quiet areas as well as active areas and try to provide boundaries between different activities. This helps to keep distractions to a minimum for certain children and gives the impression of working and playing in a smaller group.

• Provide a range of resources – for example, chunky crayons as well as finer ones, large-scale floor puzzles as well as small table-top games. Look for scissors that can be squeezed or used hand-over-hand as well as the usual types. Check that colours can be seen by any children with visual impairments – for example, yellows are sometimes easier to see than reds.

▲ ● ■ Choosing your words

Consider whether the language that all the adults in your setting use is inclusive for all the children.

• At one level, this might involve introducing other language speakers for children who speak English as an additional language.

• Make sure that you use terminology that is not based on the medical model. For example, you would never say, 'that chicken pox child', so try not to say 'that cerebral palsy child' or 'that SEN child'. Otherwise, you are conveying the message that the child is representative of the condition rather than an individual. Remember the maxim, 'child first, condition second'.

• You will need to keep your language and gestures simple and clear when communicating with most children who have additional needs. Sometimes signing can be used alongside language to get the message across or to help the child communicate meaning.

• Choose your words carefully, emphasising key words and gradually increasing vocabulary, perhaps linking words to actions or real objects.

• Use positive language, telling a child what to do (for example, 'please come down') rather than what not to do ('stop climbing').

• Don't bombard with questions – try providing a simple commentary as you play alongside the child instead. Communicate in any way that you can and make sure that communication is kept enjoyable and successful.

▲ ● ■ Involve children in celebrating their own progress

It can be discouraging for children with additional needs and their parents or carers if their progress is blatantly much slower than the other children's. Try to convey the message that you value the child for what they can do, whatever that might be. When you are recording progress, make comparisons against the child's own starting points and needs rather than against a common 'norm'. In that way, you can share and celebrate progress for that child. After all, what constitutes a small step for many of the children in your setting might be an enormous step for a child who has additional needs. Through your knowledge of the individual child and your experience in children's development, try to spot those 'golden moments' that constitute real progress for that particular child and keep careful observations of what happened, what led up to it and what you will move on to next. You will find a photocopiable sheet for recording an individual child's milestones and progress on page 62.

Through your knowledge of the individual child and your experience in children's development, try to spot those 'golden moments' that constitute real progress for that particular child.

Meet the Children

In this chapter, you will read about the range of additional needs you might need to support in your setting.

▲ ● ■ Areas of additional need

Each child is unique and we should be wary of generalisations. Remember that you do not need a medical diagnosis in order to assess and meet a child's additional needs.

Once you have got to know the child as an individual, talked with parents or carers and tuned in to how that child plays and learns, it might be helpful to know a little more about the range of needs covered. This will increase your awareness about what the barriers might be and what approaches are often successful for supporting a child's needs.

The SEN Code of Practice talks very broadly about children having needs and requirements which may fall into at least one of four areas:

• communication and interaction;
• cognition and learning;
• behaviour, emotional and social development;
• sensory and/or physical.

The activity books in this series each address an area of additional need. The needs chosen reflect the areas most sought after by readers of the earlier SEN series: Autistic Spectrum Disorders; Speech and Language Difficulties (both aspects of communication and interaction) and Behaviour, Social and Emotional Development. In this chapter, we will look at these additional needs and also find out more about children with other kinds of disability and SEN. But remember that your best source of information is the parents and carers, the SENCO and any other professionals already involved. Each child is unique and we should be wary of generalisations. Remember that you do not need a medical diagnosis in order to assess and meet a child's additional needs.

Communication and interaction

▲ ● ■ Autistic spectrum difficulties

Some things to note:

• Some children appear indifferent to other people and behave as if they are 'in a world of their own'. They might have been diagnosed as having 'autism', 'autistic features' or 'Asperger's syndrome'. All these conditions have some overlap.
• Those who are significantly affected may not play with other children and join into activities only if an adult insists and assists.
• They might have very little language, they might echo what is said to them, or they might talk a lot about topics of great interest to them.
• Sometimes, they might become absorbed in arranging toys in a certain way, collecting certain objects, or spinning or turning toys repeatedly to watch them move.
• Their eye contact might be very poor and they might be unable to play imaginatively, unless it is in a very stereotyped way.
• Their behaviour might be bizarre or very fearful, especially if familiar routines are disturbed or if they feel stressed.

• Many Local Authorities have a specialist teacher or team available to advise you – ask parents or carers for information.

There are plenty of ideas, strategies and activities to help these children in the book *Inclusive Practice in the Early Years – Autistic Spectrum Disorder* also in this series.

▲ ● ■ Speech and language difficulties

Some things to note:

• Some children's speech and language development is 'delayed' but nevertheless progressing along normal lines. Perhaps these children are delayed in other areas of their development as well, and the language delay is just one part of this immaturity.

• Other children lack the ability to make certain sounds or cannot coordinate the sounds in the required sequence. These children are sometimes described as having 'dyspraxic', 'dysarthric' or 'articulation' difficulties.

• Some children cannot speak clearly, or their language remains rather like a telegram.

• For others there is a specific language 'disorder' which means that they would benefit from specialist therapy and approaches to reorganize their language processing. For these children, their understanding of language (their receptive language) is usually affected as well as their use of language (their expressive language).

• If the child's difficulties are significant there is likely to be a speech and language therapist involved – ask parents or carers for information.

There are plenty of ideas, strategies and activities to help these children in the book *Inclusive Practice in the Early Years – Speech and Language Difficulties* also in this series.

Cognition and learning

▲ ● ■ Developmental delay

Some things to note:

• All children vary widely in the age at which they reach various developmental stages. It is quite normal to have a wide variation in your setting.

• However, some children fail to achieve their developmental milestones within the usual time range and are sometimes described as being 'delayed' in their development.

• For some children, there might be a clear cause – perhaps they have a chromosomal condition such as Down's syndrome (see opposite) or perhaps they have not yet had the necessary early years experiences in which to learn and to develop.

• For others, there may be no known cause; it is simply that a child seems to be taking longer than other children to progress.

• Some children will catch up eventually; others may continue to have learning difficulties. The help that you should provide is the same.

• If the child's developmental delay is significant, there might have been a Portage Home Visitor involved in the past – ask parents or carers for information.

• You will find all the strategies for differentiation on page 31 especially helpful for supporting children with developmental delay or other learning difficulties.

▲ ● ■ Down's syndrome

One baby in about 1000 is born with Down's syndrome. It is caused by an additional chromosome in each body cell. The word 'syndrome' means a collection of signs and characteristics. All people with Down's syndrome have certain facial and other physical characteristics. However, it is important to realise that there are far more differences between people with Down's syndrome than similarities. Each child is an individual in his or her own right and we need to respect this.

Some things to note:

• Children with Down's syndrome usually have greater difficulty learning than the majority of children their age.

• Many children with Down's syndrome are healthy, but 40% have heart problems at birth and some might need surgery. There is also a much higher risk of hearing difficulties, vision needs careful monitoring and there is a tendency towards more frequent infections and 'chestiness' too.

Behaviour, emotional and social development

▲ ● ■ Attention difficulties and ADHD

Some things to note:

• Some children have attention difficulties which are greater than for other children their age. This is because they have a physiological difference in their brains controlling their arousal system. It can be helped through careful behaviour management and also sometimes through medication (such as Ritalin) once they are older.

• In the Early Years, these children may or may not have been diagnosed as having 'Attention Deficit Hyperactivity Disorder' (ADHD) and there are two reasons for this. Firstly, most children in the Early Years are highly active at least some of the time (most settle down as their concentration develops). Secondly, medication should not be prescribed until the child is old enough to have a say in how the medicines makes them feel – usually about age six. This is because the side effects can be unpleasant and the medication may also suppress appetite.

• It makes more sense for you to identify that a child has difficulties in attention and concentration and plan the best approaches to help. You do not need a diagnosis to do that.

▲ ● ■ Behaviour difficulties

Some things to note:

• If a child has had time to settle with you and is not responding to your normal encouragement and boundary setting, then you might consider talking to parents about using approaches which are additional or different to usual – these are the children who you would describe as having 'behaviour difficulties' and who would benefit from being on your SEN approaches and having a within-setting individual behaviour plan.

There are plenty of ideas, strategies and activities to help these children in the book *Inclusive Practice in the Early Years – Behavioural, Emotional and Social Difficulties* also in this series.

▲ ● ■ Emotional difficulties

Some things to note:

• Emotional difficulties in children can take many forms and can stem from many sources. It is most important to address these early in order to prevent mental health problems developing later on.

• Sometimes children seem extremely shy and continue to cry or to be withdrawn long after you feel they should have settled with you.

• Sometimes you will have children who continue to find it very hard to separate

from their parents and carers and become very distressed on arrival and also when it is home time.

• Others cannot seem to cope with newness, with failure or with correction. They might destroy their own work or creations as if they did not matter and behave as if they were not bothered by your praise and encouragement. These children are often described as having very low self-esteem.

There are plenty of ideas, strategies and activities to help these children in the book *Inclusive Practice in the Early Years – Behavioural, Emotional and Social Difficulties* also in this series.

Sensory needs

▲ ● ■ Hearing impairment

Some things to note:

• Many early years children suffer from temporary, fluctuating, or even permanent hearing loss.

• Some children are born with a permanent hearing impairment, and many more will have a temporary loss caused by colds leading to ear infections.

• Other children have a build-up of mucus in the middle ear which stops the sounds being transmitted properly, leading to 'conductive deafness'. This is known as 'glue ear' and is often treated at hospital by draining the mucus and then inserting grommets.

• 'Sensori-neural deafness' usually means that sounds are not being processed correctly in the inner ear. Sometimes this can follow rubella during pregnancy, mumps or meningitis. This is likely to be a permanent hearing impairment.

• In 'mixed deafness', children may have a mixture of conductive and sensori-neural hearing impairment. Very few children are totally deaf.

• Some children need hearing aids to amplify sound. Cochlear implants are a kind of hearing aid that sends electrical signals to the brain. Radio aids help you to communicate clearly to the child even if there is background noise.

• Children with hearing difficulties often miss out on important vocabulary and will need extra support to develop concepts and to make links in their thinking and playing.

• If a child's impairment is significant, there is likely to be a specialist teacher for the hearing-impaired involved who can advise you.

▲ ● ■ Visual impairment

Some things to note:

• Some children have difficulty in seeing people and objects clearly unless they are close up and well-lit. They are severely near-sighted or 'myopic'.

• Some children can only see clearly at a distance. They may be severely far-sighted or 'presbyopic'.

• Some children have difficulty in coordinating the movement of their eyes when tracking and need patches to make one eye more dominant.

• Some children cannot identify between different colours; 'colour-blindness' can take different forms.

• Some children have patches of blindness or even tunnel-vision which restricts their field of vision.

• Some children's sight is so restricted that they are effectively 'blind'; about 5% of children with visual impairment go on to use Braille for reading and writing.

• If a child's impairment is significant, there is likely to be a specialist teacher for the visually impaired involved who can advise you.

Physical needs

▲ ● ■ Physical difficulties

Some things to note:

• Children who have physical and coordination difficulties have a wide range of needs. Some might have mobility difficulties and are not yet walking. Others may have 'fine-motor' problems and find it hard to dress, hold a pencil or make small finger movements.

• Sometimes this will be because of a recognised condition such as cerebral palsy or spina bifida.

• Sometimes it will be because their physical development is delayed for their age on account of other developmental difficulties.

• Sometimes they are 'clumsy' and their coordination is still immature, perhaps because they have a specific learning difficulty such as 'dyspraxia'.

• Some children will have been given special equipment to help them sit, stand, move and balance.

• There will usually be a physiotherapist or occupational therapist involved who can give you advice – ask the parents or carers for information.

▲ ● ■ Cerebral palsy

About 1500 babies are born with cerebral palsy every year in Britain. It is caused when part of the child's brain is not working properly so that body movements cannot be coordinated by the brain.

Some things to note:

• Cerebral palsy is not a degenerative illness, but a condition that can be worked on with therapy and encouragement so that the child is affected as little as possible.

• Symptoms might be very slight, or so severe that the child needs help in every day-to-day task. Movements may be slow and awkward, floppy or stiff, poorly controlled, and sometimes unwanted.

• You must never assume that, because children have considerable physical difficulties, they will also be slow in their thinking and intelligence.

▲ ● ■ Developmental dyspraxia

Some things to note:

• Children whose development of motor coordination is impaired are sometimes described as having 'Developmental Coordination Disorder' ('DCD' sometimes known as 'dyspraxia').

• The diagnosis is usually only made if the impairment significantly interferes with educational progress or daily activities.

• These children appear to be clumsy in their movements. They find it hard to learn how to move and balance smoothly. They may also be poor in organising themselves, find it hard to speak clearly, and find it difficult to understand where their body is in space.

• Compared to other children their age, these children may find it hard to dress and undress in the setting, have a poor pencil grip, find jigsaws and puzzles hard to do, and be poorly balanced when running or climbing.

• There is usually no particular cause or neurological impairment, and it is thought that dyspraxia is related to an immaturity in the brain rather than to any damage. It can therefore usually be improved with practice, with maturity and with exercises.

▲ ● ■ Spina bifida

The condition of spina bifida is present from birth and affects the child's physical and neurological development.

Some things to note:

• The amount of disability depends on how greatly the spinal cord is affected, where the bifida is, and the amount of nerve damage involved.

• Often there is paralysis below the fault, with incontinence and a difficulty or inability to walk.

▲ ● ■ Getting to know you

Remember that you do not have to be a specialist in any of these conditions in order to support a child's needs. There should be other professionals to help and support you and your SENCO should be able to tell you who these people are and how you can access them. Above all, talk with parents and carers and get to know the child as an individual. This will help you to see 'child first, condition second'.

> Above all, talk with parents and carers and get to know the child as an individual. This will help you to see 'child first, condition second'.

Following the Code

In this chapter, you will find a summary of what the SEN Code of Practice advises you to do when supporting young children with SEN.

▲●■ The SEN Code of Practice

The definitions of 'special educational need' and 'learning difficulty' have not changed since the 1996 Education Act and are provided in the SEN Code of Practice (DfES 2001). You should have a copy of the Code in your school or setting and it shows clearly which are statutory requirements and which are guidance. The SEN Code of Practice is your 'bottom line' when it comes to meeting SEN. Most of you will already be very familiar with it by now but, for the purposes of new SENCOs and those of you who have not worked with SEN before, this chapter has a general summary.

Basically, a child has special educational needs if he or she has a learning difficulty which calls for special educational provision to be made. Also a child has a learning difficulty if there is: a significantly greater difficulty in learning than the majority of children of the same age; a disability which means that their needs cannot be met locally; or is under five and would certainly have a learning difficulty if special educational provision were not made. Special educational provision for a child over two means any educational provision which is additional to, or otherwise different from, the educational provision made generally for children of the child's age in the local authority and, for a child under two, educational provision of any kind.

▲●■ Who is the Code for?

All foundation stage classes in English schools (including independent schools) and settings registered to receive government funding must have regard to the SEN Code of Practice. There are equivalent codes and regulations in Wales, Scotland and Northern Ireland. The Code is not just for settings who already have children with SEN. There are certain requirements

even if you do not have a child with SEN attending. For example, you should have a clear policy about how you will meet SEN in your setting, agreed by the management group or governors and with the involvement of practitioners and parents. You should also be able to demonstrate that you 'have regard to' the SEN Code of Practice and that systems are in place for identifying any child who might have SEN. You should also appoint one member of staff who is familiar with the requirements of the Code of Practice and who can act as a point of contact for parents, staff and the LEA. This person is called the special educational needs coordinator or SENCO. You will read more about the SENCO's role in Chapter Five.

▲ ● ■ Keeping individual records

You should already be keeping information for all the children using your ongoing assessments and observations of each child's progress within the EYFS. What additional records do you need to keep for a child who has SEN? The pupil record for a child who has SEN should include information about the child's progress collected from your own observations and assessments within the setting, from parents and carers and from any outside professionals involved where this is relevant to your support. What are the child's own perceptions of her or his difficulties? What strategies have been used to ensure that the child has access to the EYFS? How have these worked? What are the child's strengths and weaknesses?

The welfare requirements of the EYFS say that you should have effective systems in place to ensure that the individual needs of all children are met and that you need sensitive observational assessment in order to plan for their needs. The activity books in this series show how you can start with the Learning and Development grids that are suitable for all children and then refine these more sensitively in order to observe, plan and record for children who have SEN and might be learning differently. The welfare requirements also specify that you must keep a record of the children's SEN status – whether they have no SEN, are on Early Years Action, Early Years Action Plus or have a statement of SEN. You will read about all of these phases of SEN below.

▲ ● ■ Early Years Action

It is recognized that good practice can take many forms and early years providers are encouraged to adopt a flexible and a graduated response to the SEN of individual children. This approach recognizes that there is a continuum of SEN. Some children's SEN will be met simply by your adapting your approaches and targeting the learning more carefully. Others may require higher levels of support and differentiation and you might need to bring on board specialist expertise if the child is experiencing continuing difficulties.

Once a child's SEN have been identified, the providers should intervene through Early Years Action. When reviewing the child's progress and the help they are receiving, the provider might decide that more support is needed and therefore to seek alternative approaches to learning through the support of the outside support services. These interventions are known as Early Years Action Plus. This does not mean that assessment should be seen as a linear process, moving from Early Years Action to Early Years Action Plus. Instead, assessment and intervention should be appropriate to a child's individual needs at any particular time, each review of the process informing and feeding back to the next.

You need to have faith that the interventions you plan can manifestly work. Do not be tempted to feel that if you have identified a child's SEN then it requires an SEN expert to deal with them. Your expertise is early learning and this is precisely what the child needs access to. Most of children's SEN will actually be met within the setting, without direct recourse to outside expertise. Early Years Action can and does work and many children will only spend a temporary period on SEN approaches. However, other children with more long-term and complex needs may go on to require more specialist input or provision.

> Do not be tempted to feel that if you have identified a child's SEN then it requires an SEN expert to deal with them. Your expertise is early learning and this is precisely what the child needs access to.

▲ ● ■ Initial concerns

If you feel a child has SEN, you should gather information about the child from any other professionals involved and make the play and early learning activities more accessible to the child by breaking them into smaller steps or making them easier. The activity books within this series provide you with practical ideas about how this can be done. You should also speak with parents; this becomes easier if you have shared progress from the beginning and developed a welcoming and positive atmosphere for the families who attend. You should ask parents for further information about the child's health, development or behaviour at home as well as in the setting, and tell their group's SENCO about your concerns so that he or she can share ideas and approaches. Some settings have found that the term 'special needs' can be rather daunting for parents, and instead have explained that they would like to 'monitor a child more closely' for a while in order to help them make progress and meet their 'additional needs'. There is an 'initial concerns form' on page 55 which you might like to adapt or photocopy. Enter the names of the children that you are monitoring more closely and add the decision made after a period of early intervention. The decision you make might be that you are no longer concerned and therefore do not need to adopt approaches that are additional or different to usual. Alternatively, it might be that you have all come to realise that you should plan Early Years Action to provide that child with more support.

The SENCO and the early years practitioner will then be in a position to consult with parents and agree an Early Years Action aimed at enabling the young child with additional needs to reach maximum potential. This usually involves individualized teaching by the practitioners and individualized learning on the part of the child. It will not usually mean one-to-one teaching and this might not be appropriate if the child is to be included fully in the EYFS. Staff can then work closely with the child, following the plan that has been agreed, observing and recording the child's progress, and meeting with parents and the SENCO to review progress. Parents and carers must always be kept fully informed of their child's progress.

> Parents and carers must always be kept fully informed of their child's progress.

▲ ● ■ The individual education plan

A feature of this individualised approach is the individual education plan or 'IEP'. You should meet regularly as a team with parents to negotiate the IEP, term by term, or more frequently if you feel it is necessary. The plan should lead to the child making progress and should be seen as an integrated aspect of the curriculum planning for the whole group. It should only include that which is additional to or different from the differentiated early years curriculum that is in place for all the children. Differentiation of the planned activities (see page 39) will make the curriculum accessible to those children who have SEN. There are various ways of writing an IEP and practitioners need to develop a style that suits their situation and meets the requirements above. There is a photocopiable form for you to use or adapt as an individual education plan on page 56, written from the point of view of a child.

▲ ● ■ Top tips for writing IEPs

Try to move away from using labels as explanations and explain the barriers that a child faces instead.

Individual education plans should be a key feature of planning for any SEN in your group, either as part of your Early Years Action or your Early Years Action Plus. They are also used regularly for children who have statements of SEN. As you will know, they should contain three or four short-term targets and they must include clear information on how you will know that your teaching has been successful. Bearing in mind our definition of SEN, they only include that which is additional to or different from the regular early years curriculum that is in place for all the children. So, what can you do to make it more likely that the IEP will become a practical, working document that will result in positive progress being made by the child?

• IEPs are usually drawn up by the practitioner working directly with the child rather than the SENCO, though the SENCO should support and advise if necessary. They are much more likely to be used as working documents if those at the 'coal face' have been involved in their creation.

• Try to involve parents and carers in drawing them up so that they are negotiated and agreed between you. This gives a much stronger message about partnership than presenting them at review as 'something I made earlier' simply to be rubber stamped.

• Try to move away from using labels as explanations and explain the barriers that a child faces instead. For example, instead of recording Jamie's difficulty as 'Down's syndrome', explain that, 'Jamie sometimes finds it hard to learn new concepts and skills'.

• As well as recording the difficulties and barriers that the child faces, make space to record the strengths. This helps you to build on the strengths in order to support the weaknesses.

• Think through all the wording you have used. If this was your own child, would it all sit comfortably with you?

• Try to use your words to paint a picture of the real child. Though this is an official document, try to give real examples and use descriptive words that bring the child to life to the reader.

• Aim for just three or four targets. Keep them short and simple and make sure they are S.M.A.R.T. (specific, measurable, achievable, realistic and time-bound). For example, 'By the end of this term, Annabelle will be able to count to five and pass me five cars on request'.

• Only include targets for those Areas of Learning affected by the child's SEN. The rest of the time, that child should not need approaches that are additional or different from usual.

▲●■ Regular reviews

The IEP needs to be reviewed regularly. There is a photocopiable review form which you might like to use or adapt on page 57. You can also ask parents and carers to contribute, using the form on page 58. Sometimes, after reviews, you might feel that a child is still not making the progress that might be possible. Perhaps you have planned approaches and monitored these with parents over several review periods, but the child is not achieving the targets you have set. You should first revisit the targets you have set and make sure that you have broken them down sufficiently for the child to make progress. If you feel that you have exhausted your ideas and resources, you might decide together that the time has come to seek outside professional help. Parents need to be in agreement, and this kind of decision would normally arise out of one of your regular review meetings. Usually, parents are very happy to seek outside help if you put it to them that you yourselves need more advice and support in helping their child. Try not to give the message that you are asking for outside help in order to label their child or to confirm that their child is 'different' in some way. After all, about a fifth of all children are going to need individualised approaches at some stage of their school careers.

▲●■ Early Years Action Plus

If you decide to call in an outside agency for more advice, assessment and support and if this advice then contributes to the child's IEP, this is known as Early Years Action Plus. Some children entering an early years setting may already be at this stage. Who is actually involved and the kinds of advice available will vary with local policies and practices. Most children's services within the local authority have early years support staff who are available for general advice and support. Find out who you can approach for advice and what the referral mechanisms are. It is good practice never to share information with another agency unless parents and carers have given you written permission. You will read more about working with other professionals and agencies in Chapter Eight. Even though outside professionals might be involved, the SENCO continues to take a leading role, working closely with the member of staff responsible for the child.

▲ ● ■ Requesting a statutory assessment

For a very few children (only those requiring a very high level of support or a specialist placement), the help provided by Early Years Action Plus will still not be sufficient to ensure satisfactory progress, even when it has run over several review periods. The provider, external professional and parents may then decide to ask the local authority to consider carrying out a statutory assessment of the child's SEN. In most authorities, the SENCO needs to consult a support teacher or educational psychologist from the support services first. They will advise on completing the necessary forms and ensure that all the relevant evidence in support of a request is attached. A special form is usually needed, countersigned by parents. Sometimes it is parents themselves who write to the local authority and request them to consider initiating a statutory assessment. Parents can seek further information about this from its Parent Partnership Service.

It is helpful if this information is attached to any outside referral or request to a local authority for statutory assessment:

- copies of IEPs;
- evidence of the implementation of the IEP within the EYFS and whether it was effective;
- any reports concerning the child's general development and health, perhaps from the health visitor or school nurse;
- the notes from previous review meetings;
- reports from any outside professionals;
- any written views of the parents and carers.

▲ ● ■ Statutory assessment

The local authority must decide quickly whether or not it has the evidence to indicate that a statutory assessment is necessary for a child. Parents and other professionals involved will probably receive letters from the local authority asking for their views on whether or not a statutory assessment should be made. If it decides that it does not have enough evidence, then it will write to you explaining why a statutory assessment has not been initiated. Do not feel too despondent if your request has been turned down. It might be simply because you have not provided sufficient evidence. Make sure that the local authority has sight of all your planning, seeking advice from the support services if you feel that your planning was not targeted carefully enough. If you are still concerned after another review period that a statutory assessment should be considered, then you can contact the local authority again.

If the local authority decides to proceed with a statutory assessment, then it is responsible for coordinating this. It will call for the various reports that it requires, from an early years teacher (usually a support teacher, early years practitioner or EYFS teacher), an educational psychologist, a doctor, and a social worker if involved, and will ask parents or carers to submit their own views and evidence. The doctor (usually a school doctor or community pediatrician) collects together any reports and evidence from other health service professionals involved such as a speech and language therapist or physiotherapist.

Over this time, parents will receive a number of formal letters from the local authority. These can be rather daunting, but the authority is required by law to send these. It is often helpful if you can reassure parents about their contents and put them in touch with an independent parental supporter (IPS) or parent partnership officer (PPO) if they need explanations or have concerns or queries. A phone call to your local authority will inform you of the names of the 'IPS' and 'PPO' for your area.

▲ ● ■ What happens next?

Keep your language simple, relevant, objective and try again to 'paint a picture' of the real child that shines through all the paperwork!

The statutory assessment follows strict time guidelines, and if the early years setting is approached for a report, then a strict time for returning it to the local authority will be given. The whole statutory assessment procedure must not take longer than six months unless there are exceptional circumstances which are defined clearly in the full text of the Code of Practice. Your role becomes one of continuing to meet and monitor the child's needs in the interim, to help support the parents or carers through the process where appropriate and to submit any useful assessment information as part of the process.

If you are asked to provide a written report, you will be given advice about what your report should contain. Keep your language simple, relevant, objective and try again to 'paint a picture' of the real child that shines through all the paperwork! You can do this by providing real examples for the evidence you quote. You will need to gather all the assessment information you have for the child. Your setting is in a unique position to provide information about how the child is learning and developing over a continuous period of time. Only you can provide evidence of where the child is learning within the EYFS and of what approaches have proved problematical or effective. Remember that everything you write will be shared with parents, carers and other professionals.

▲ ● ■ Statements of SEN

The statutory assessment may or may not lead to a statement of special educational needs. When it has gathered all the evidence, the local authority might feel that a statement is necessary because of the special educational provision required. Parents have various rights of appeal to an SEN tribunal if they are not happy with the statutory assessment procedures, and these are also fully covered in the SEN Code of Practice. The independent parental supporter can advise parents on their rights and choices. A statement of SEN states what the child's special needs are, what provision will be made for them, how the needs will be monitored, and where the child will be placed. It is the responsibility of the authority to name the setting which the child should attend, taking parents' views into account. Sometimes, a local authority decides that there is not sufficient evidence for a statement and writes a 'note in lieu' instead. This is rather like a more formal IEP and will be implemented and monitored by the setting.

▲ ● ■ Supporting children who are statemented

If your setting is named as the child's placement, then you will need to see a copy of the child's statement. If your setting is part of a split placement for the child, then each setting needs to keep closely in touch with each other to share planning, progress and expertise, working closely with parents at all times. Even though the child has a statement, it is still your role to continue to meet and monitor the child's SEN as you did before, though this will now be with the support and provision named on the statement. Usually this will involve regular contact with a member of the support services, helping you to set the child's IEPs and to review progress. Sometimes, additional equipment or perhaps additional hours of support are provided to help the child in the setting or to help staff with EYFS planning. If a child has a statement of SEN, it does not follow that there will be additional hours of support provided. It all depends on the child's needs and what the local authority decides is appropriate to meet those needs. The local authority will ask the SENCO to call regular (usually six-monthly) reviews to monitor whether the child's needs are being met. A six-monthly review cycle (or even less) is recommended for children under five because their needs change so rapidly at this stage.

Identifying and Supporting SEN

In this chapter we look at how to identify SEN within the broad framework of the EYFS and introduce the assessment-planning-evaluation model used in the activity books in this series.

▲ ● ■ Disability discrimination

There is now a disability discrimination law which applies to all early years settings whether or not they are in receipt of a government nursery grant. Disability is defined as a physical or mental impairment which has a substantial adverse effect on the child's ability to perform normal day-to-day activities and is likely to last more than a year. Any blanket policy that you write for inclusion must make sure that no disabled child is treated 'less favourably' and must show how you make 'reasonable adjustments' for disabled children. Always keep careful records of why you reached the decisions that you did and what you considered along the way. For example, you should not deny a child a place in your group if they are not toilet-trained because of an underlying condition or developmental delay. Also, you cannot exclude a child with a condition such as autism because of their difficult behaviour, if this was clearly related to the condition and if you did not take steps to reduce stress, manage behaviour and meet SEN. When you are expecting a child to join your setting, think through the session in detail and collect all the information that you will need to be able to make reasonable adjustments to your spaces, your approaches, your routines and your activities. You will find plenty of suggestions for planning suitable adjustments and interventions in this series.

▲ ● ■ The importance of early intervention

The importance of early identification of special educational needs is highlighted in the Code of Practice for SEN. The earlier that action is taken, the more responsive the child is likely to be, and the more readily intervention can be made without undue disruption to the child's education. If a difficulty proves to be temporary, then the child will make good progress during your interventions and will be able to learn and progress in the usual way in the future. If the child's difficulties prove less responsive to your SEN interventions, then an early start can be made in considering the additional provision that may be needed to support the child's progress.

You need to make a distinction between identifying specific conditions and identifying SEN. You are likely to be a specialist in identifying SEN because you will have been trained and you are hopefully experienced in working with children in their early years. However, you are not a specialist in diagnosing conditions and neither do you need to be, as there are other services available to do just that, should the need arise. You do not need a medical diagnosis or a recognized condition in order to plan for SEN. Instead, make a practical decision based on whether a

> You do not need a medical diagnosis or a recognized condition in order to plan for SEN. Instead, make a practical decision based on whether a child requires additional or different approaches in order to make adequate progress.

child requires additional or different approaches in order to make adequate progress. Remember that, in an inclusive approach, 'child' will come first and 'condition' second.

▲ ● ■ Keeping records

As an early years practitioner, you are likely to find yourself in one of two situations. Either, you are welcoming a child into your setting whose SEN have already been identified – in which case you plan your approaches along the line of the SEN Code of Practice explained in Chapter Three. Otherwise, you might be wondering whether a child already with you has SEN and whether you should therefore take steps to identify these and begin to plan for them. This can seem daunting at first, but if you remember that your role is to work out which children need additional or different approaches rather than to identify a condition or to diagnose, then you will realise that you are the right person to do this job. You will never be alone. You must work alongside parents and carers who will already have a wealth of information on their child. There will be the SENCO to give you specific advice and support and hopefully outside professionals ready to give general guidance.

▲ ● ■ Ongoing observations

What kind of evidence should you gather if you feel that a child might have SEN? Checklists suggesting developmental ages and stages can be useful sometimes, though each child follows a unique pathway to development, so they can only be used as a broad guide. They might suggest to you that a child's physical development, for example, is 'six months delayed from the norm' but do not tell you why or what you might do about it. Besides which, what is normal for different children varies widely. Ongoing observations are far more important and relevant. There are some general ideas for what to look out for below and also in the introductions to each chapter in the activity books.

• During your ongoing assessments and observations of all the children, always record the who, the when and the where so that you can look back and note how a child managed in small- or large-group activities, in structured or freer learning situations and in child-initiated or adult-led play.

• Keep notes of how the child learns best. For example, is it first thing in the morning, when there are no visual distractions or with certain other children?

• What help or prompts are needed for the child to be able to learn new skills?

- Make notes of interesting staff/child dialogues and provide the context.
- Keep observations of how the child plays and interacts with other children, again recording the context as well.
- Note how the child approaches new situations and new learning.
- How helpful is it when you provide clearer guidelines to play and behaviour or when you provide 'scaffolding' for the child's learning – in other words, how teachable is the child?
- Are there certain activities and playthings that are regularly chosen or avoided?
- Keep examples of the child's creations and work (with the child's consent) or use photography to record these.
- Note how the child responds to his or her own work and creations or what the child says about them.
- Keep notes of any discussions with parents and carers.

You can monitor your initial concerns on the photocopiable sheet on page 55, sharing your concerns, plans and reviews with the SENCO. Together with the parents and carers you will then be in a better position to decide whether to move into the SEN arrangements outlined in Chapter Three.

▲ ● ■ Starting to differentiate

> As soon as you share some initial concerns about a child's progress, start to differentiate your activities and play experiences so that the child has a chance to make better progress given your support.

Differentiation (or breaking steps down) should not wait until you decide that a child has SEN. As soon as you share some initial concerns about a child's progress, start to differentiate your activities and play experiences so that the child has a chance to make better progress given your support. There are plenty of ideas for differentiation in Chapter Six and also in the activity books from this series. For many children, it could be that a period of differentiation is all that is needed to develop the skills necessary to make better progress. In this case, you will monitor your initial concerns for a while and then conclude together that this child does not have SEN and that you can meet their needs without having to plan Early Years Action. For other children, you might decide that a high level of differentiation and support will be needed for longer, specifically targeted to the child's needs in certain Areas of Learning. In this case, you will need to take the steps necessary to plan SEN approaches through Early Years Action, working in partnership with parents and carers.

▲ ● ■ Using the activity books

This series suggests a practical approach for removing some of the barriers that children with SEN might face, based on open-ended planning and play plans. In the next sections, we describe what this approach looks like and explore an example of how it might work.

All effective planning flows from ongoing assessment and observation and is subject to monitoring and evaluation. At the beginning of each activity chapter you will find a general introduction to that particular focus of play, followed by a developmental assessment sheet. This photocopiable sheet allows you to observe and record what a child with particular SEN can do at the moment in terms of their development within the EYFS framework. There will clearly be skills and competencies that the child demonstrates already almost all of the time. There will be others that are demonstrated sometimes, depending on the child's mood or level of confidence, who they are with and the particular context of the day. There will be others still where the child has not demonstrated that skill or competency at all. This 'always/sometimes/never' recording method enables you to make a very simple assessment of the starting points for your teaching and support, concentrating on behaviours that the child demonstrates sometimes, though not always. By starting your interventions at the level of 'emergent skills', both you and the child concerned have a greater chance of success and progress.

▲ ● ■ Using the play plans in the activity books

In each practical chapter of the three activity books in this series, you will find a two-page assessment record showing the skills and competencies linked to the focus of learning. Six of the skills or competencies on each assessment record have been asterisked and correspond to 'play plans' that you can adapt and use with the child to support that skill or competency. In this way, you are using the assessment to identify starting points for teaching and support and then selecting a plan that will help you all get started. Some of the play plans can be dipped into in any order to suit your circumstances and some need to be followed in a specific order – these are clearly marked by a logo suggesting that you 'dip in' or 'follow the sequence'. Of course, each play plan is written in general terms and you might need to adapt it or even develop your own more personalised plan, depending on the needs of the particular child. For this purpose there is a blank template at the back of each activity book. There are also blank spaces within the existing plans to develop your own personalised approaches.

▲ ● ■ Monitoring progress

When you are using the play plans from the activity books, make use of highlighting to flag up interventions that you wish to focus on or use dating and initials to record who has applied each intervention and when. Each book contains a monitoring sheet to help you record how your play plan or intervention went; what you did, how it worked and what you plan to go on to next. Monitoring sheets are an excellent way to share progress with parents and carers and you can use the assessment/play plan/monitoring framework as a useful way of involving the family in your interventions. Outside professionals should recognise the steps that you are working through on your assessment sheets and can provide you with more specific and personalised advice if the child you are working with has more specialist needs.

▲ ● ■ Reflective practice

In each activity chapter in the three activity books in this series, you will find ideas for how you can observe (using the 'look, listen and note' format of the EYFS) and how you can plan effective practice. This way of thinking should already be familiar to you through your knowledge of the EYFS guidance. However, you might not have had previous experience of applying the principles to children who have particular SEN and the ideas in each activity chapter will show you how to do this. Reflective practice involves thinking carefully about what you are doing and adjusting what you do in light of your findings. In order to do this in your work with children with SEN, you will need to tune in to their particular needs and what makes them most ready to learn, learn how you can plan approaches in the light of your discoveries and then evaluate how effective your interventions have been. We hope that you find the format suggested in this series easy to use, effective for the children concerned and a helpful way of developing your reflective practice.

▲ ● ■ Using the activity books

Here is an example of how the approach was used for Prasarn who is four and has a diagnosis of autistic spectrum disorder (ASD). His teacher looked through the Areas of Learning in the EYFS framework and decided, based on what she had found out about ASD and about Prasarn, that there were some areas he would have great difficulty in accessing. One of these was the focus on 'Dispositions and attitudes' within the Area of Personal, Social and Emotional Development. She then looked at the typical developmental stages that children might progress through towards those Early Learning Goals and talked to the SENCO about the typical barriers faced by children with ASD.

For example, under 'Dispositions and attitudes. She looked at how Prasarn might signal his likes and dislikes to other people, given that he tended to play 'in a world of his own'. She came up with these stages that she would like to see Prasarn progress through.

She then drew up a simple play plan which she shared with colleagues, looking at how they could all encourage the first steps in this plan, working towards one of the targets in his IEP. She was able to share this with Prasarn's aunty who supported him at home.

▲ ● ■ You need support too

If you are going to meet each child's needs inclusively, there are bound to be times when you yourselves need the support and advice of other professionals to do this. Try to see anyone else's involvement as a partnership rather than a 'take over'. If you feel that a child has SEN, do not assume that it needs the experts 'out there' to provide all the assessment and intervention because you are not specialist enough to do this. You are already a specialist in how young children learn and develop. Use your existing knowledge and expertise in delivering the EYFS framework to identify strengths and weaknesses. This knowledge will help you to create strategies for supporting and helping the child, and your knowledge and expertise will allow you

> If you are going to meet each child's needs inclusively, there are bound to be times when you yourselves need the support and advice of other professionals to do this.

First steps for Prasarn

Signalling his likes and dislikes

- First he will behave in a way that allows us to interpret his likes/dislikes.
- Then we would like him to indicate a choice by grasping.
- Then to indicate a choice by looking at it.
- Then to indicate a choice by pointing at something.
- Perhaps in future to indicate a choice using words.

to monitor how effective you are being. The first point of contact for all early years practitioners should be the setting's SENCO and in Chapter Five you will read more about this role and the support that a SENCO might provide.

Prasarn's Play Plan

Area of Learning: PSED   Focus: Dispositions and attitudes

Individual target: Behave in a way that shows what I like/dislike.

Observe Prasarn during free play and note down his choices and length of time with each activity.

Observe what makes Prasarn happy, sad, angry, anxious, bored (and so on) using photography and descriptions. Make this into a communication book to share with colleagues and family.

Offer a choice of two playthings at once for Prasarn to look towards, reach for, point to or ask for.

Try to teach a yes/no response by asking 'Do you want this?' and holding up one toy at a time. As Prasarn selects, emphasise 'YES – this one!'

Try to share Prasarn's favourite game, moving in to play at the edge. Share your enjoyment in it so that Prasarn can see and hear how you express your pleasure.

Offer a choice of drinks/playthings/snacks in succession, helping Prasarn to give you a yes/no response after each item.

Introduce phrases like: 'Which does Prasarn like?'; 'This is Prasarn's favourite!'; 'Prasarn doesn't like this one!' Use your tone of voice and expression to emphasise the feeling.

Gather favourite playthings into a special box for Prasarn. Try to alternate playing with something from the favourite box with something else. Don't force this and provide plenty of support, showing Prasarn how to play.

The Role of the SENCO

The special educational needs coordinator or SENCO plays a key role in ensuring that children with SEN have their needs identified and met early. SENCOs support their colleagues in planning effective interventions, making reasonable adjustments and organising inclusive and flexible activities for all.

▲●■ Who is the SENCO?

The SENCO works closely with the head of the setting and colleagues, and has responsibility for the day-to-day operation of the setting's SEN policy.

All registered settings and schools should also appoint one member of staff who is familiar with the requirements of the Code of Practice and who can act as a point of contact for parents, staff and the local authority. For small settings, the special educational needs co-ordinator (SENCO) might also be the play leader or one member of staff with a particular training or knowledge of special needs. For private and voluntary providers it is often the room leader, manager or deputy manager. For school foundation classes, the SENCO is often shared with the rest of the school.

▲●■ What does a SENCO do?

The SENCO should:

• act as a contact for other members of staff in interpreting the SEN Code of Practice and for training;
• support colleagues in identifying and meeting the SEN of children within the setting;
• oversee records kept on SEN for individual children;
• act as a first point of contact for the parents and carers, the local authority, health services, social workers and others on SEN matters;
• seek outside advice and support if needed, for children in the setting or those about to join it;
• ensure that parents or carers of children with SEN are kept informed and consulted throughout;
• put other members of staff in touch with relevant SEN training so that they can identify and plan early for any SEN.

▲●■ Following the Code

The SENCO works closely with the head of the setting and colleagues, and has responsibility for the day-to-day operation of SEN procedures in the setting. All registered settings must have an SEN policy agreed with governors or the management committee. It is good practice if this is drawn up with the full consultation of colleagues and parents. Once in place, it becomes the responsibility of the SENCO to see that this is

> Being a SENCO is a responsible and rewarding job and you need training, support from your line management and an element of protected time in order to do the job properly.

put into practice on a daily basis and to monitor how effective it is. In Chapter Three, you will have read about the various phases of meeting SEN under the SEN Code of Practice and it is often the SENCO that makes sure that this works smoothly. For this reason, the SENCO is often to be found:

• working with colleagues to monitor any initial concerns;
• deciding with colleagues and parents when a child might be said to have SEN;
• working with colleagues to draw up the IEP;
• providing advice to colleagues on how to plan interventions and plan support for a child with SEN;
• calling review meetings and liaising with parents and carers (and sometimes chairing these meetings and writing them up afterwards);
• organising any referrals to outside agencies with parents' agreement;
• liaising with the local authority concerning any statutory assessments and statutory reviews.

It is sometimes tempting for settings to leave all the work of meeting SEN to the SENCO but this is not in the spirit of the SEN Code of Practice. Interventions are most likely to be put into practice when planned by those who work directly with the child, though leaning on the experience and guidance that the SENCO should be able to offer. The SENCO's duties and responsibilities all take considerable time if they are to be done properly and ideally this needs negotiating with the manager or headteacher. Being a SENCO is a responsible and rewarding job and you need training, support from your line management and an element of protected time in order to do the job properly.

▲ ● ■ The inclusion policy

One way to bring together all the policies that you need for inclusion, SEN, equality of opportunity and behaviour, anti-discriminatory practice, behaviour and anti-bullying is to provide a full 'inclusion policy'. Bearing in mind that you need to be wary of blanket policies and therefore need to tease them apart in order to identify those aspects that are specifically relevant to your setting, below are some starting points for things to include and consider when designing your own SEN or inclusion policy.

1. Your inclusion policy

How do you define 'inclusion' in your setting or school? Offer your definition and then explain that this policy describes what you do in your setting to make sure that all children can participate, belong and develop, whatever their background or level of ability. The policy should also describe how you aim to communicate and share information with the parents and carers from your local community.

2. Your aims

Presumably you aim to provide a setting where each and every child feels accepted and valued. Write down what you believe. For example, perhaps you want each child to feel happy and to grow in confidence, whatever their needs.

3. Who the policy is for

You might state that the policy is for all staff members (including those not directly involved with educating and caring for the children, all managers and all those who have been vetted to work on a voluntary basis with you).

4. The children covered

Hopefully, you believe that each and every child has a right to be included. However, you might need also to point out that you understand that certain children might need closer support and encouragement than others. Mention those children for whom you are keen to provide an inclusive service. For example:

- children who have SEN or other disabilities;
- children for whom English is not their first or only language;
- children who belong to minority groups;
- children who are vulnerable because of their behaviour or the behaviour of others.

You might mention that in your setting, you already welcome children with a range of SEN and that there are several languages spoken by the families who attend.

5. Your inclusion co-ordinator

Perhaps in your setting you have one person who makes sure that this policy is put into action on a daily basis. In the past, the person responsible for meeting SEN was the SENCO. In some settings, this role is widening to include other aspects of inclusion, for example, making sure that people with disabilities have the best access possible, ensuring equality of opportunity, making sure that no-one is discriminated against, and seeing through your behaviour policy. This person might be called your 'inclusion coordinator'. Mention who it is and how to make contact.

6. Meeting SEN and supporting children with disabilities

Explain how you identify and support children with SEN in line with the SEN Code of Practice and the Disability Discrimination Act. You might include a shortened version of Chapter Three of this handbook in your policy. Explain that the inclusion coordinator (or SENCO) gets to know all children who have needs that are additional or different and acts as a first contact for parents, carers and outside professionals. The inclusion coordinator also advises staff on their approaches and interventions, though it is the responsibility of each staff member to actually meet the child's needs on a day-to-day basis. Include in your policy the names of members of staff who have had training in SEN and any specialist training, experience or resources available in your setting or school.

7. Outside agencies

Include a mention of the outside professionals that you currently receive input from. Discuss how contact is made. Do you always obtain written consent from parents and carers before sharing information with others?

8. Physical access

What adaptations have been made to your premises to make them more accessible? Perhaps you have made adaptations to allow disabled parents to deliver and collect their children or made sure that your toilet facilities are suitable for children with physical disabilities.

9. Managing transitions

What do you do when a child with additional needs transfers to another setting or school? How do you make plans for the transition and who is involved? What information is passed on and to whom?

> It is the responsibility of the inclusion co-ordinator or SENCO, with the support of the manager or head teacher, to keep up to date with new guidance and legislation concerning inclusion.

10. Avoiding discrimination

Mention what you do to ensure anti-discriminatory practice. Perhaps all staff members meet annually to discuss their inclusive practice, examine their own attitudes and beliefs and make sure that their practice is anti-discriminatory to all the children, families and visitors that you work with.

11. Promoting positive behaviour

Since this series includes a book on planning inclusive activities for children who have BESD (*Inclusive Practice in the Early Years – Behaviour, Emotional and Social Difficulties*), you might like to combine your behaviour policy with your SEN policy by including a section on behaviour in your broader 'inclusion policy'. Consider starting by saying that you want all the children to develop friendly and helpful behaviour and not feel bullied by others. Now state how you aim to do this, perhaps mentioning some of the approaches in the BESD activity book (see above) for planning inclusive activities for children with BESD. What do you do if a child does not respond to your usual approaches? Perhaps you discuss the situation with parents or carers and then design an individual behaviour plan to suit the child, based on positive approaches. Mention the outside professionals who are there to help as well.

12. Preventing bullying

If anyone is concerned that a child is being bullied, who should they discuss it with initially? What steps do you take? What do you do if these do not work? How do you know whether the children you look after feel safe and secure?

13. Evaluation

You need to evaluate annually how successful your inclusion policy has been. How will you do this? For example you might examine the level of diversity within your setting, talk regularly with parents and carers and obtain their views, monitor how successfully any additional and different needs are being met, consult with the children about how they feel about coming to your group and consult staff members on how supported and successful they feel in helping each and every child to participate.

14. Keeping up to date

It is the responsibility of the inclusion coordinator or SENCO, with the support of the manager or headteacher, to keep up to date with new guidance and legislation concerning inclusion. Each year the inclusion policy should be brought up to date in light of these changes, in light of the children's needs and views and after consultation with staff, governors or the management committee, parents and carers.

▲ ● ■ Supporting colleagues

If you are named as the SENCO within your setting, it might seem daunting at first. Do not worry that you are not a specialist in different medical conditions – you should already be knowledgeable about or experienced in how young children learn and develop. Your main role is to support your colleagues in using common-sense and child-centred methods to identify and intervene with SEN, to serve as a contact for parents, carers and other professionals and to find things out when you don't know.

Planning Inclusive Play

In this chapter, there are ideas for breaking steps down and planning inclusive play experiences for children who have SEN.

▲ ● ■ Issues to consider

The Learning and Development Requirements of the EYFS state that all Areas of Learning should be delivered through planned, purposeful play, with a balance of adult-led and child-initiated activities. This raises two important issues for those of you working with children who have SEN. The first is that many of your adult-led structured activities may be too challenging for a child with SEN to access. How can you break steps down so that the children can succeed and make progress, despite their SEN? The other issue concerns play that is child-initiated. Since children who require a high level of support might actually be disadvantaged in terms of being able to make friendships and to learn from other children, what can you do to ensure friendships and self-initiated play for these children, despite any SEN? These are the two issues considered in this chapter.

The importance of differentiation

The process of breaking down learning steps to make them more accessible to children who have SEN is known as differentiation. It is especially useful when you are planning adult-led and structured activities for the children. You will see many examples of how to differentiate learning in the play plans in the activity books of this series. Most methods of differentiation are based on certain basic ideas which you can read about below. If you can understand these basic principles, then it should help you to apply differentiation to all kinds of learning situations, whatever the nature of SEN or activity.

▲ ● ■ Content

> It is important to build on children's strengths if they are to cope more successfully with the content of what is on offer.

It is important to build on children's strengths if they are to cope more successfully with the content of what is on offer. The content of the story, for example, may need to be simplified so that it is at a level appropriate to the child's stage of language or understanding. You might need to include concrete props to hold attention, emphasize the meaning of key words and allow a child to participate with more than one sense at once – looking, listening and doing.

▲ ● ■ Pace

Allowing the child extra time to respond, or ensuring opportunities to get there first, are ways of building confidence. Activities may be presented at a slower pace to ensure understanding or a succession of materials presented to maintain interest during a discussion. Some children need to 'sandwich' short periods of structured activity with periods of free play or quiet. Some children take a long time to process information, and need longer silences than usual if they are to answer a question or fulfill a request. Others may find it hard to remember more than the last piece of information given to them and therefore need supporting and prompting at each step, taking longer to carry out structured activities.

▲ ● ■ Level

All planning within the EYFS will include a degree of planning for different levels of children's ability. Within this, it might be that some children need the learning steps broken down more finely, and it may be necessary to give value to a smaller and less obvious learning outcome. Within the activity books of this series, there are many examples of how to break Early Learning Goals down into step-by-step developmental sequences. The size of step depends on the degree and nature of the child's difficulty and the barriers faced. In practice, you might find yourself having to break steps down into much finer stages for certain children with SEN. You do this by observing what a child can do now and assessing what approaches and step sizes work best – this is more effective and personalized than rigidly following a fixed checklist.

▲ ● ■ Resources and equipment

Think about the way in which materials and resources are presented in your setting. Can all children find and reach them when they need to? Are there genuine choices available to each and every child, whatever the SEN? Some children may need adapted scissors to cut out a picture, or require photographs rather than line drawings in order to name objects. Some might need toys and playthings which are easy to handle (such as form-boards with knobs on the pieces). Others might need table tops at a suitable height for them to access when in a standing frame. Some might need radio hearing aids to hear, or to sit close up to large picture books to see. Contact the occupational therapist or physiotherapist involved (or speak with the parents) if you feel that special equipment might remove some of the barriers preventing a child from accessing your activities.

▲ ● ■ Response

This involves the outcome produced by the child and may be linked to the level at which the activity is presented. Some children may be able to show they have learned through actions rather than words and any response that the child is able to give needs to be valued. For example, some rely on sign language to make their

sounds clear. Others may not be able to tell you their wishes, but can demonstrate by their smiles or their choices where they would like to play.

▲ ● ■ Sequence

Some children need to have opportunities provided at different times, or need to cover different aspects of a topic at separate sessions. If attention is short, it might be necessary to revisit an activity at another time in order to ensure success. Some children find it harder to settle and to concentrate after they have been very active. Others need to 'let off steam' for a while in order to return more attentively to an activity.

▲ ● ■ Structure

Some children learn best when they are playing in a highly structured setting, led and supported by an adult. Others seem to respond best when provided with free play and when they are supported in developing their own agendas. Every child needs opportunities to play and to learn both on their own terms and in groups with other adults and children.

Always seek for a balance between open-ended play and fixed learning outcomes, and between child-led play and adult-led play. You will find a mixture of all of these in the play plans included in the activity books from this series.

> Every child needs opportunities to play and to learn both on their own terms and in groups with other adults and children.

▲ ● ■ Teacher time

Some children need more individual adult support and time. This can include some one-to-one work or withdrawal into a small group, but mainly refers to supporting the child with additional encouragement and prompting within the regular group. Simply having a heightened awareness of the child's individual needs can affect teacher involvement. In an inclusive setting, any time spent relating individually to an adult would take place in the early years room itself, with opportunities for involving other children as well.

▲ ● ■ Grouping

The group structure may afford opportunities to allow the child to respond or for other members of the group to provide good models which can reinforce the child's learning. Sometimes meeting the needs of individual children with SEN has led to children working alone on individual materials, but arrangements to include the child's IEP within planning for the whole group can overcome this and lead to a more purposeful and supportive way of meeting SEN.

▲ ● ■ Type of help

Some children learn best when they see something done first, some when they listen to your instructions and some when they have a go themselves. Most young children are a mixture of all three learning styles. Children with SEN will have learning style preferences too and these can be very important to them. Use your ongoing observations to assess how they learn and make the most of their areas of strength. You will also find that some children with SEN respond well to physical prompts (for example, hand-over-hand support); some to visual prompts (watching a demonstration first or pointing a finger towards the right space on the puzzle); and some to a verbal prompt (using the adult's voice to hold the child's attention, give clear instructions or to assist recall). When using physical and visual prompts, always pair these with your language so that, in time, those children that are able to can come to respond to, your words alone.

All of these approaches to differentiation are common sense and arise from your personal knowledge and experience of the child and their needs. Taking time in the early stages to closely observe and monitor the child can help you to 'tune in' to the way in which children are experiencing their session and allow for more practical differentiation where opportunities are lacking.

▲ ● ■ Breaking steps down

Once you have decided what to encourage or teach next, use a combination of all these approaches to differentiate the learning and to plan the next steps that might be achievable for the child. Try using the photocopiable form on page 60to help you to do this and to share your step-by-step approach with your colleagues. Here is an example.

Sam is four and has BESD. He tends to behave very impulsively and to act before he thinks of the consequences. From what you know of Sam and his difficulties, you might have realised that certain sections of the EYFS Learning and Development grids are going to be hard for him. In order to make this manageable for Sam the stages need to be broken down into smaller steps.

Let's take an example – Sam is likely to be challenged by the focus pages on 'Language for thinking' within the Communication, Language and Literacy Area of Learning:

• Start by considering the 'Development Matters' stages that children typically move through. Though this should not be seen as a teaching curriculum in itself, it should give you an idea of the approximate stage that Sam has reached.
• This in turn will allow you to pick out an appropriate long-term goal for Sam such as: 'Sam will use talk to connect ideas, explain what is happening and anticipate what might happen next.'
• Once you have discussed and agreed on a goal for Sam, then you can begin to use your ideas on differentiation to break that step down into much smaller steps with the right level of support at each stage. For example, you might start with something as simple as 'Sam will tell me what might happen next during simple puppet play'.
• These steps can form the basis of a personalised play plan for Sam.

This kind of approach is exemplified throughout the activity books in this series, where play plans have been provided that break down long term goals into smaller steps for a variety of focuses within the Early Learning Goals.

The importance of friendships

We should never underestimate the importance of children's friendships and how much they can appropriately learn from one another. Adults with disabilities sometimes speak of how they were denied the opportunity to do, just this because of well-meaning but over-zealous shadowing and support from learning assistants at school. How can we balance the need for adult support with the need to be fully included with one's peers?

Here are some guidelines, as suggested by practitioners who have worked with children who have SEN in both special and mainstream settings.

First of all, friendships can be fostered through carefully managed meetings and greetings. By welcoming the children individually to the room and then encouraging

> We should never underestimate the importance of children's friendships and how much they can appropriately learn from one another.

them to join their friends on the mat, you are helping the children to greet each other. You can use this social time to draw the children's attention to each other, to point out similarities and differences and speak as if the children were able to verbalise to one another, even if a child with SEN does not have spoken language yet. Always use names and take care to focus the children's attention on their friends when talking about another child.

Research on how young children define their friends suggests that 'friends' are seen simply as those children with whom a child has spent time playing – nothing more complex at this stage. Therefore if you plan opportunities for different combinations of children to play and share adult-led activities together, you can actually breed a sense of 'friendship' amongst the children. Therefore in settings where some of the children have SEN or disability, it is particularly important to set up activities that include all the children.

▲ ● ■ Know when to 'stand back'

Hopefully, there will be many occasions when you might notice a child who has SEN playing together happily with the other children, sharing the toys or playing creatively in the home corner. This is something you might have been eagerly hoping for and one of the targets you set for the child in the IEP. Though you should celebrate this amongst yourselves, do not be tempted to interfere with what is clearly going very well for the children concerned. At the same time, you will know that certain children find it difficult to play in a sociable manner or to sustain an interaction, so you should also know when not to stand back. For example, you might step in to teach the word 'gentle' or to interpret one child's wishes or needs to another.

Your very presence at times might allow a positive interaction to carry on for much longer than it might have done otherwise, since you can make sure that there is social turn-taking and a balanced exchange. In fact, when providing additional support to a child with SEN, aim to become a 'child magnet'! By 'being available' you will inevitably draw other children, eager to share their experiences with you. This can develop into really interactive experiences in which you can act as a bridge between a child with SEN and the rest of the group, interpreting the child's reactions or behaviour and helping the other children feel that they have socially connected with each other. Do what you can to set these interactions up, but then have the confidence to stand back.

▲ ● ■ Using digital photographs

Children's photographs are a powerful way of encouraging friendships. For example, you can use individual photo albums in the book corner to catch children's interests in themselves and others and to act as talking points. Try using laminated photographs of the children at group time to mount on a felt board and to signal group membership. You can use photographs to offer social choices ('Who do you want to play with next?') or activity choices ('What would you like to do next?') Photographs are also a brilliant way for you to catch 'golden moments' on camera to celebrate with parents, carers and to talk through with the children themselves. Children's own photography provides you with an important insight into what is important to them and can act as a talking point about how included and supported a child feels.

Another strategy using children's photographs has proved very useful in signalling turn-taking on favourite equipment such as the computer. Children who have ASD sometimes find it hard to share, especially if it means leaving their favourite computer activity. Try attaching a small photo of the child concerned to the computer to signal that it is that child's turn. When the turn is over, a new child's face is attached, signalling that it is time for their turn now. You can also use huge sand timers or ringing cooker clocks to signal that in a few minutes time it will be time for something new. This helps children with ASD to prepare for change. You can also use photographs, pictures or symbols of activities to create visual time tables. These are sequences of pictures that show all the children what is going to happen next and in what order (this can be particularly helpful to children with ASD, BESD or S&LD and helps them to feel more settled within your routines).

▲ ● ■ Encouraging turn-taking

When a child with SEN first joins your setting, you might need to plan structured activities that encourage turn-taking play between that child and other children.

Early reciprocal games (involving an element of 'my turn–your turn') are a good starting point. These include games of hide and seek, chase and tag, rolling a ball between you, one child blowing bubbles for another child to pop and playing with musical instruments, leaving gaps for each other to respond. Start by teaching the rules one-to-one with an adult, and then provide support as a child with SEN attempts to play reciprocally with another child. Sometimes joint IEP targets are drawn up to encourage friendships so that staff members can work on two children learning to play together. There are more ideas for encouraging children to participate with each other in Chapter Seven.

Encouraging Participation

The key to encouraging participation is to listen closely to the children in our care. Listening to children allows us to make sure that they can participate in all that we have to offer them. It also helps us to make sure that we are meeting the needs of any child who has SEN.

Listening to children

…the process of "listening" should involve all our senses as we take active steps to encourage each and every child's participation and belonging.

Here 'listening' is used in its widest sense and involves tuning into children, seeing the world from their own points of view, offering them choices, consulting them on matters that are important to their lives and adjusting what we do in the light of their responses. In other words, the process of 'listening' should involve all our senses, as we take active steps to encourage each and every child's participation and belonging. Listening to children has been defined in *Listening as a way of life* by the National Children's Bureau as:

• An active process of receiving, interpreting and responding to communication. It includes all the senses and emotions and is not limited to the spoken word.

• A necessary stage in ensuring the participation of all children.

• An ongoing part of tuning in to all children as individuals in their everyday lives.

• Sometimes part of a specific consultation about a particular environment, choice, event or opportunity.

▲●■ Why listen to children?

Young children have a right to have their views taken into account when we plan and deliver our services:

• on equality of opportunity grounds because they are part of our community;

• on educational grounds so we can better match activity and learner;

• and on psychological grounds because we know that active involvement in play, care and learning increases success and well-being.

The Children's Act (2004) places a duty on us to work together to promote the well-being of children relating to five outcomes which were chosen in consultation with children:

• to be healthy;

• stay safe;

• enjoy and achieve;

• make a positive contribution to society;

• and achieve economic well-being.

Underpinning the *Every Child Matters* framework (DfES/1081/2004, downloadable from www.everychildmatters.gov.uk) is the notion that children are integral stakeholders in their own learning, social and health care. In order to plan effective services we need to take their views into account as well as those of other people.

▲ ● ■ Seeking feedback

Knowing how successful we have been in our delivery of the EYFS and in meeting SEN under the SEN Code of Practice involves seeking feedback from the children and families concerned. Therefore another reason for listening to young children is because they make better progress if they are fully involved. Children carry important and relevant information about their likes, dislikes, strengths and needs. Their support is crucial to the effective implementation of any intervention. We can better match the opportunities we provide to the children's level of play and development if we provide them with real choices and adapt what we do in the light of their decisions. The SEN Code of Practice (2001) makes it clear that staff in settings registered to receive government funding must look for ways of involving children with SEN in your planning and intervention.

▲ ● ■ How we can listen to young children with SEN

> We understand that children tell us things in many different ways – through their voices, but also through the way they behave and the feelings they express.

There are many ways in which you can listen to and consult with young children, including those who have SEN or those who might not be able to express themselves in words. Below is a general overview of some of the approaches.

• Children as individuals. We can listen to young children by getting to know each of them as an individual. Children are more likely to communicate their needs, opinions and feelings to us if we have already established a relationship with them. We are also better able to interpret what they are telling us if we know them well. We understand that children tell us things in many different ways – through their voices, but also through the way they behave and the feelings they express.

• Children's likes and dislikes. We can also listen to children by establishing their likes and dislikes. We can do this simply by observing children at play, by offering choices and noting children's selections, through asking the children to record what they like and dislike on camera or by talking together in groups, through simple questionnaires or on a one-to-one basis. We could gather information about children's likes, dislikes and how they make their needs known on entry into a service or setting using a simple 'welcome profile' to gather information (see below). For children who have SEN or a disability, this becomes especially important. You will find an example of a simple 'child passport' on page 61 in which new carers are helped to interpret a child's feelings from their expressions and behaviour and to respond accordingly.

• Children's art and craft work. We can listen to some young children through their art and craft work. We do this by giving them chances to draw and paint and to talk to us about what they are doing. Children's drawings can be talked about together and used to find out about a child's interests and feelings. For example, when children with BESD have strong feelings or memories, they might try to express these through their paintings. By talking to them about their creations, we give them a chance to talk about their feelings too.

• Use child-held cameras. We can find out what is important to children by using child-held cameras. Adults can obtain a child's-eye view of nursery life by providing a camera and encouraging a child to take photographs of the things that are important to him or her. Practitioners can then piece together a picture of children's priorities and impressions by collating evidence from the children themselves and adding the views of parents and nursery colleagues. These can be built into a book or portfolio that can serve as a record of the child's achievements for the future. For children with complex SEN, the adults themselves can observe the child and catch 'golden moments' in photographs to celebrate progress.

• Use picture and story books. We can use stories and picture books as a means of introducing situations and encouraging talking. Early years settings often build up useful collections of stimulus books for covering a range of new situations that the child might meet; going to hospital, having a new baby in the family or living with one parent. We can also use picture books to discuss strong feelings with children who have BESD or to introduce disability and ethnic diversity. It is important that the books that we provide portray images of diversity in natural everyday contexts.

• Imaginative play. We can encourage imaginative play as a way of introducing situations and encouraging talking. For example, we can use themed play to create new experiences for children – such as going into hospital or how to make friends – so that they have a chance to share their feelings and learn new social skills.

• Use resources that reflect diversity. By providing toys, resources and picture books that reflect a wide diversity, we allow each child to participate and to express themselves. Listening to what children have to say on equality issues shows us that even the youngest children in our settings start to learn about what is different, as well as what is similar, between people. They begin to form values and responses to these differences by observing other people's behaviour and can be sensitive to how children are included or excluded. Children are more likely to feel included and to make their voices known if practitioners make sure that the teaching materials and books within the early years setting reflect a wide range of ability, ethnicity, and culture. Picture books which contain 'models' of differently abled children can act as talking points.

• Consult the children. For children who have SEN, we can involve them more fully by consulting them about their IEPs. Take a moment to consider the points at which children could be offered choices or asked for their views during a busy session. These can range from simple choices about where, how and who to play with, through to what they need to learn next and how to go about it. Practitioners should use their knowledge of the individual children to ask or establish how they feel about their individual education plan, whether they feel comfortable with it, and how they would like to contribute. Make sure, when you are planning additional support, that you do not deny a child the opportunity to play with other children and the opportunities that this creates for learning from each other.

• Offer choices. We can also listen to children by making sure that all children can make real choices in their play. Offering choices allows children to direct their own play, provided that practitioners have thought ahead and planned suitable and

enjoyable learning experiences for the menu. If a child has additional needs, then we need to make sure that there are 'real' choices on offer by removing any barriers to learning and play. For example, if a child cannot use words to communicate, they need to be offered actual playthings and activities to select between. Symbols, pictures and objects of reference, such as a spade to suggest sand play or a cup to suggest drinks time, can also be used to encourage pointing, an eye glance or a yes/no response.

Using observations

As well as listening to children it is also vitally important to spend time observing them as they play and interact with others. Use your regular observations (perhaps with photography) to monitor the children with SEN as they select activities and initiate play. You can learn a great deal about how involved children are in their play and note some of the more complex links that children develop as they combine one area of play with another. Children's learning rarely fits the neat boxes that adults like to define! Your notes and photographic 'audits' of how equipment, areas and activities are regularly used can also be a useful tool in deciding which to adapt or replace in order to present that aspect of the EYFS in a more appealing way.

> As well as listening to children it is also vitally important to spend time observing them as they play and interact with others.

▲ ● ■ Childwatching

Whilst it should be easy to 'tune in' to children who can talk to us and tell us their views and feelings, it can be more of a challenge to tune in to babies or children who have complex disabilities and cannot speak. 'Childwatching' is an approach which allows practitioners to reflect on the non-verbal children in their care and how they can participate more fully. It uses child observations and the writing of a 'child's day' narrative to help staff members tune into children with SEN in their care. The process helps staff members to modify what they do in order to encourage more listening and participation.

The process involves three steps. First the room leader or SENCO carries out a running observation of a child's day or part day in the setting. This is then written up as a narrative story describing the day through the eyes of the child, if the child could talk. All names are changed and the interactions are jumbled up so that it remains anonymous. Finally, staff members then reflect on the narrative during a structured feedback session. They discuss how they would like to modify their own behaviour in order to encourage better 'listening' to the child concerned and therefore ensure the child's fuller participation in the activities of the session.

▲ ● ■ Observing the very young

One setting used the 'Childwatching' method to observe the level of participation of very young children in their baby room. They came out with the top tips opposite for improving baby participation (which are as appropriate for all babies as they are for children with complex needs).

Top tips for encouraging participation in the very early stages:

- Pause for a moment to observe a child before you interact.
- 'Listen' to the child's behaviour and what they want to do.
- Follow the child's lead where appropriate.
- Examine your resources to make sure you can give the child adequate choice.
- Extend on resources for particular Areas of Learning or SEN.
- Make sure visual stimulation is at the child's level.
- Prepare and engage the child's attention before putting on bibs, wiping faces and so on.
- Cut down on adult-to-adult interactions in front of the children.
- Try not to keep coming in and out of the room!
- Enjoy each other – that's why you chose this job!

Written records

Writing down and recording your notes and observations allows you to share all that you have learned about the children – their views, their wishes and their SEN with other colleagues and carers. This, in turn, allows others to 'tune in' more closely to the children's needs and encourages greater participation and belonging.

▲ ● ■ All about me

It is helpful if you can put together a description of the child with SEN in simple terms, perhaps written as the child would if they could do so. This can be shared between home and setting and can be a quick way for new adults to get to know a child's needs and how they communicate and play. You can either do this yourself (and there is a photocopiable version on page 61 to use or adapt) or make use of a published version. For example, there is a useful pamphlet 'All about Me!' that forms part of the PEAL training materials (see page 63). Within it, there are pages for:

- a parent or carer to enter names and photographs of important people in the child's life;
- important things that staff members should know about the child;

And in the child's voice:

- things I like to do at nursery;
- things I do not enjoy at nursery;
- things that make me happy about starting school;
- things that make me worried.

There is also an 'All about me' booklet available which is a checklist that enables parents to note down and record from time-to-time their child's development and progress. It covers seven areas of the child's life and experience;

- language,
- playing and learning,
- doing things for myself,
- my physical development,
- my health and my habits,

- other people and how I behave,
- my moods and feelings.

Though it started as a parent record, it was adopted by many schools and early years settings as part of improving a child's sense of participation and belonging.

▲ ● ■ Welcome profiles

We might use child-centred questionnaires or interviews that a parent or carer completes when their child first joins the setting in order to get to know a child quickly. Open-ended questioning is best since it allows a parent or carer to be open about what their child needs and does not beg a certain reply. For example: 'Tell me a favourite toy/activity/family outing/memory…'; 'Is there anything which makes your child particularly worried?'; 'How much help does she need when going to the toilet?, or, 'How does he let you know when he is cross/happy/upset?'. This allows you to gather honest information about all children regardless of their ability. Some settings have involved the children in designing and illustrating these to make an attractive document to share with new parents and carers.

▲ ● ■ Child passports

One way of helping colleagues to tune into and include children who have severe and complex needs and who may not be able to communicate with you clearly is to develop a 'child passport' for them. In your passports you might include pages on 'All about me'; 'Friends and family', 'Nursery and interests', 'The physical stuff' – any special equipment and aids needed, communication, eating and drinking, medical information, contact numbers and action in emergencies. The organization 'Kidzaware' has produced one you might look at (the 'Pocket passport' from www.specialabilities.co.uk) and there is also information available through SCOPE (www.scope.org.uk).

Sometimes it is useful if the communication section of the passport stands on its own as a separate book. This is particularly the case if a child's disabilities are such that it is difficult for those unfamiliar with him or her (such as new staff members, babysitters or other parents) to understand how he or she makes their needs known. For example, Oscar's family put together a 'Communication Book' for him because he is still in the early stages of developing language. It is laminated for easy handling and can hang from his wheelchair wherever he goes. The passport allows Oscar to communicate his needs quickly to those who are just beginning to become acquainted with him. It contains a series of captions and photographs showing Oscar in various moods and explains how to 'read' his appearance and how to respond. For example, there are photographs to show 'This is me when I am happy' or 'There is something happening here that I don't like – maybe a loud noise or a new experience.' And 'When I look like this I like to be cuddled.'

Working with Others

Working in partnership with parents, carers and other professionals is at the centre of the SEN Code of Practice and the EYFS framework. In this chapter we examine what 'parent partnership' means in practice.

▲ ● ■ Working with parents and carers

Practitioners need to listen to what parents have to tell them, making sure they have clearly understood what they are being told.

This lies at the heart of inclusion and makes absolute sense. Yet it can still raise challenges for those of us working with families, especially if the family or children concerned have additional or complex needs. The term 'parent partnership' has been around for the past 30 years but what does it mean in practice? There are many ways of working in partnership with parents – examples include, consulting parents in the design of the building, discussing plans for the admission policy, developing services and provisions, recruiting staff and ongoing management issues (through governing bodies and committees). As you can see, this can operate at many different levels and involve whole authorities and communities as well as individual settings. For the purpose of this chapter we will focus on how practitioners can work in partnership with parents or carers in order to support more parental involvement in their children's learning and development – both at home and in the setting, and particularly when that child has additional needs.

What do parents and carers need from us if we are to work in partnership with them? Firstly, we must recognise that parents and carers are a huge resource to us in terms of the amount of insight and information they carry about their children's needs. Practitioners need to listen to what parents have to tell them, making sure they have clearly understood what they are being told. The parents' and carers' existing knowledge of their children must be valued, and the contribution that they have already made to their child's development must be acknowledged. At the end of the day, parents need to have increased confidence in what we have to share with them and it is vital that they are left with the feeling that they still have some choices and control.

Parents and carers usually like to become active partners in solving problems. They like to be encouraged and given hope. They do not want to be judged and must never be told that 'you're getting it wrong'. They might indeed welcome help, but not in a way that suggests that the practitioner is the one with all the answers and expertise. They might wish to work with someone they can trust who can signpost them to the right services and give them practical and workable advice. All this involves sharing common aims with parents, working together, sharing our complementary expertise and developing mutual respect for each other.

▲ ● ■ What gets in the way of partnership?

All of this takes time and therefore needs to be given a high priority – it needs planning for at all levels. From the parents' perspective too there can be constraints arising from various pressures: work, financial concerns, other children or family members, language barriers, cultural differences, negative experiences of their own schooling, negative experience of previous professionals, a lack of understanding of how play and learning link together, parents' own health issues or disabilities, literacy levels, low confidence and simply a different attitude ('it's the nursery's job, not mine'). For parents of children with additional needs, there might also be very strong feelings bound in with sharing their child's care with someone else – a genuine difficulty in 'letting go' and a genuine fear that you will not cope with their child. We will explore some of these complex feelings next.

▲ ● ■ Parents of children with disabilities

> Having a young child who is disabled or who has additional needs carries a whole set of additional stresses and strains which make early support and parent partnership more important than ever.

Having a young child who is disabled or who has additional needs carries a whole set of additional stresses and strains which make early support and parent partnership more important than ever. It helps if early years practitioners can try to 'tune in' to some of the emotional reactions that they might be picking up from a parent.

• There may be feelings of guilt: 'What did I do wrong?' or 'Are they telling me I'm doing things wrong?'

• There may be an inclination to apportion blame: 'They caused this difficulty' or 'They are doing this wrong'.

• Another common strand is a strong feeling of wishing to protect their child, especially if that child needs a very high level of care: 'Can they cope like I've been coping?'

• There may be very natural feelings of anger: 'Who does she think she is, telling me there's a problem here…?'

• Grief is an almost universal reaction: 'If we stop to talk about this, I'm afraid I might cry. Best to avoid it.'

• Most parents feel helpless in some way, at least initially: 'Can I cope with the fact that I've now got to share my child's care with someone else at nursery?' or 'Can I bear to lose control?'

• There is a tendency at first to deny what is happening: 'I know they're worried about my child so I'll rush off before anyone has a chance to talk to me'; 'It will all be all right – there's not a problem'; 'He's just like Uncle Frank was'; 'It's just the way she is.'

• It is also with a mixture of deep shame that some families might find themselves in a state of revulsion that their child is 'different' in some way: 'I don't want to be the sort of person who has this sort of child. So I'll act as if it's not happening'; 'I'm not willing to label him' or 'I don't want her to be treated any differently from the rest.'

• Most often, there is a whole melting pot of emotions that co-exist and only serve to confuse parents and practitioners alike. The fact is that parents cannot help this and you should not take any strong emotional reaction in a personal way.

▲ ● ■ Strategies that help parent partnerships

So what can early years practitioners do to foster successful partnerships with parents and carers? There are a number of things that can be done to help ensure good relationships. Here are some of them:

Make sure that you are up to date with the support services available in your area and the SEN procedures that you should be following.

- Allocate a key person to support the child and become a contact for parents and outside professionals.

- It is helpful if parents and carers are involved in the early years sessions wherever possible so that they can see what the setting is trying to achieve. As well as sharing the activities, practitioners can share the reasoning behind them and an idea of how their child might develop next. They can also share some of their enthusiasm and excitement about the way children play and learn and try to pass on skills.

- When talking to parents, avoid using responses such as 'I know how you feel' (as you never can) and use expressions such as 'I think I understand' instead, reflecting back to a parent what you think has been said.

- Avoid using jargon and expressions that may be meaningless to the parents. Talk in a way that they can clearly understand, and be available to help them to demystify some of the jargon that they may have heard elsewhere. Ask them if there are any words or expressions that they have heard that they would like clarified.

- Take time to share the good news of progress and to develop a positive relationship with parents before you need to share the challenges.

- Anxious parents need practical workable advice, but not the impression that the professionals are the successful ones – and they, the parents, are failing.

- Parents with low self-esteem and high stress are quick to pick up the fact that they are 'not doing it right'. This leads to resentfulness and avoidance. Instead, home-school activities should be negotiated.

- Meeting together regularly to negotiate the IEP for a child with additional needs should also bring parents firmly and practically on board with the plans for their child.

> Meeting together regularly to negotiate the IEP for a child with additional needs should also bring parents firmly and practically on board with the plans for their child.

▲●■ Early Support

There is still a wide variation in the professional services available for children who have additional needs in different parts of the country. There is a recent initiative called Early Support that aims to encourage professionals to work in partnership with parents and carers and with each other when supporting children under four with disabilities (see page 8 for contact details). The hope is that, as the Early Support materials and approaches are taken up by more authorities, the good

practice established during a child's first three years will gradually permeate upwards as the child grows older. If you are working with a child who has additional needs and is known to many different professionals, there might well be a lead professional already involved whom you can contact for further information. Always obtain written permission from parents and carers to obtain and share information about their child. If the child has more complex needs or disabilities, then there is likely to be a key worker involved who will be a useful link for you when you are welcoming that child into your setting. That key worker should already be in touch with all the other professionals involved and there might also be a Family Service Plan in place where the child's targets have already been negotiated with the family and shared across agencies. You will also find a wealth of useful information about disabilities and conditions, designed for sharing with families, on the Early Support website (www.earlysupport.org.uk).

▲ ● ■ Working with other professionals

Working with outside professionals is a feature of Early Years Action Plus (see page 25) and the correct person to call on will vary from area to area. Find out from your local Children's Centre or Local Authority Children's Services who your local support professionals are, how they can help you and how you might contact them. Most authorities have advisory teachers/practitioners or Area SENCOs to help you. There will also be educational psychologists and specialist advisory teachers for conditions such as hearing impairment, visual impairment and autism. Within the health

service, there will be speech and language therapists, occupational therapists, physiotherapists and a range of community and specialist doctors who might be involved with the family. Your best point of contact is, of course, the parent or carer who can tell you who they see with their child and what for. Just because a child is being seen by an outside professional does not mean that you should automatically monitor their needs as Early Years Action Plus – it depends if that outside involvement is contributing to the IEP. For example, a child might be seeing a speech and language therapist for help in speaking more clearly but, since their difficulty does not create a barrier in their early learning, this will not mean that they have SEN.

▲ ● ■ Voluntary organisations

Do not overlook the enormous amount of support and information that the voluntary organisations can give you. Most provide information pamphlets and websites on particular conditions, worded by parents and carers and therefore reflecting real life. The National Children's Bureau has an excellent library of resources and contacts and the organisation 'Contact a Family' aims to put parents and carers in touch with each other and to provide helpful information about all kinds of conditions. You will find contact details of useful organisations on page 8.

SEN Monitoring: initial concerns

Name of setting: ....

Name of SENCO: ....

Name	Date of birth	Date of concern	Key person	Areas we will monitor	Action we will take and by whom	Review date	Decision

Individual Education Plan

My name is:

I was born on:

My needs are being met by:
Early Years Action/Early Years
Action Plus/Statement of SEN

My additional needs are:

I need help with:

My strengths are:

Help from my parents
or carers:

This is the action planned to support and
include me:

And this is who will do what:

How we will know when I have been successful:

My targets:

1 ....

2 ....

3 ....

4 ....

When the IEP will be reviewed: ....

Who will be invited to the review meeting: ....

Signed by SENCO: .... **Parents/carers:** ....

Date: ....

Progress review

My name is:

I was born on:

My needs are being met through: Early Years Action/ Early Years Action Plus/ Statement of SEN

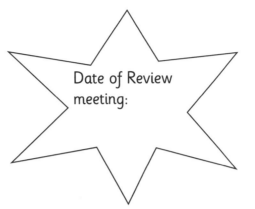

Date of Review meeting:

Who was present?

Who has sent reports (attached)?:

Since we last met, I have made this progress:

These are times when I still need support:

This is the additional support I have now:

This is how it has worked:

These are recent changes in my situation:

Have the targets on my previous IEP been achieved?

Please attach my current IEP to show my next targets and the support you will give me.

Date of next review meeting: ....

Signed by SENCO: .... **Parents/carers:** ....

Date: ....

Contribution to review from home

Dear

It would be really helpful if you could share with us how you feel we are doing with our support for .... We are planning a review meeting in the setting on: .... at .... and do hope you can come. Please let .... know if there are any problems.

At home

When does your child need most help at home?

What does your child enjoy most at home?

Are there any changes at home we need to know about?

About the setting

Is your child happy to come to us?

Are you worried about anything to do with the setting?

How do you feel about your child's progress here?

Do you feel your child's needs are being met here?

Health

How has your child's health been lately?

Are there any changes in medication or treatment?

The future

What would you like to see your child learning to do next?

Are you worried about anything in the future?

What questions would you like to ask at the review?

What changes would you like to see following the review?

Individual SEN monitoring sheet Use this table to monitor how your interventions went.

Name of child:.. Key person:...

Area of Learning:... Focus:..

Individual target:...

What we did	How the child responded	Next steps

Inclusive Practice in Early Years **Handbook**

Step-by-step planning sheet

Name of child: ....

Nature of difficulty: ....

Area of Learning: ....

Focus: ....

Target: ....

Steps along the way	Date achieved
1	
2	
3	
4	
5	
6	

Resources and support needed:

....

....

....

....

Help from parents:

....

....

....

....

All about me

Use this with parents and carers to introduce a new starter to colleagues.

My name is: ....

Here is my photograph:

My key person is: ....

These are the important people in my life: ....
....

This is what you need to know about me ....
....
....

These are things I like to do ....
....
....

Theses are things I worry about or don't like ....
....
....

I need help when ....
....
....

But I can do this all by myself ....
....

Inclusive Practice in Early Years **Handbook**

How am I doing?

Use this sheet to share my progress or to share what I have been enjoying in the group.

My name: ....

Starting date: ....

I can ....
....
....
....

Date: ....

I can ....
....
....
....

Date: ....

I can ....
....
....
....

Date: ....

I can ....
....
....
....

Date: ....

I can ....
....
....
....

Date: ....

I can ....
....
....
....

Date: ....

I can ....
....
....
....

Date: ....

I can ....
....
....
....

Date: ....

I can ....
....
....
....

Date: ....

Resources

Equipment suppliers and publishers

- Acorn Educational Ltd (equipment and resources including special needs), Tel: 01536 747485 www.acorneducational.co.uk
- Don Johnston Special Needs (produce the *Solutions for Pupils with Special Needs* resource catalogue, full of intervention resources), 18/19 Clarendon Court, Calver Road, Winwick Quay, Warrington WA2 8QP www.donjohnston.co.uk
- LDA Primary and Special Needs catalogue (products include the Jenny Mosley Circle Time Kit with puppets, rainstick, magician's cloak and many props for making circle time motivating). www.ldalearning.com
- Lucky Duck Publishing Ltd (send for a catalogue of videos, SEN books and resources, especially for behavioural and emotional difficulties), Tel: 0117 947 5150 www.luckyduck.co.uk
- The Magination Press (specialises in books which help young children deal with personal or psychological concerns). Books distributed by The Eurospan Group www.eurospan.co.uk
- Super Stickers (for reward and motivation), PO Box 55, 4 Balloo Ave, Bangor, Co.Down BT19 7PJ.
- 'Tiny Talk' baby signing and DVD' www.tinytalk.co.uk

Leaflets, books and publications

- Kidzaware produce a 'Pocket passport' for children with special abilities. Tel: 01924 385977 www.specialabilities.co.uk
- The 'Listening as a way of life' leaflets: *Why and how we listen to young children* by Alison Clark; *Listening to young disabled children* by Mary Dickens; *Are equalities an issue? Finding out what children think* by Nicky Road; *Supporting parents and carers to listen: A guide for practitioners* by Julie McLarnon; *Listening and responding to young children's views on food* by Anne-Marie McAuliffe with Jane Lane (downloadable through the National Children's Bureau website www.ncb.org.uk).
- *Developing an Inclusion Policy in your Early Year Setting* by Hannah Mortimer (QED) www.qed.uk.com
- Music Makers: Music circle times to include everyone by Hannah Mortimer (QED) www.qed.uk.com
- *Listening to young children: The Mosaic approach* by Alison Clark and Peter Moss (National Children's Bureau) www.ncb.org.uk
- The Parents, Early Years and Learning (PEAL) materials by Helen Wheeler, Joyce Connor and colleagues, (National Children's Bureau (2006) in association with Coram Family, Camden and Sure Start). Available from www.ncb.org.uk
- *Disability Equality in Education/UKDFfEA* (Disability Equality in Education) www.diseed.org.uk
- Barnado's Child Care Publications have a catalogue of useful publications, Barnado's Trading Estate, Paycocke Road, Basildon, Essex SS14 3DR.

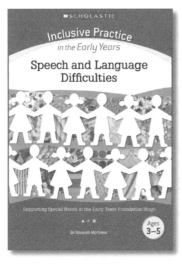
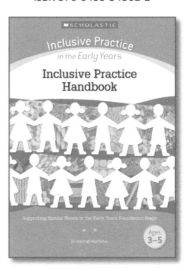

SCHOLASTIC

Inclusive Practice
in the Early Years

Inclusive Practice Handbook

Supporting Special Needs in the Early Years Foundation Stage

The 'Inclusive Practice in the Early Years' series will help all practitioners to plan and deliver activities that contribute towards the early learning goals for all children and yet carry specific targeted learning outcomes for children with special needs. The activities are also linked to the Early Years Foundation Stage (EYFS) and therefore cover a broad age range from 0-5.

The Inclusive Practice Handbook offers:

▲ Essential support to meet the requirements of the Code of Practice and the new EYFS

● Inclusive play activities that can be adapted and personalized for all children

■ Advice on developing an inclusion policy for your setting

◆ Observation and planning sheets to facilitate work with parents, carers, other professionals and agencies

Dr Hannah Mortimer is a chartered educational psychologist who has written extensively about inclusion issues.

ISBN 978-0-439-94563-9

9 780439 945639

£15.00

www.scholastic.c